ILLUSTRATED SOURCES IN HISTORY

SLAVERY
The Anglo-American Involvement

William Wilberforce (1759-1833), The Great Abolitionist

ILLUSTRATED SOURCES IN HISTORY

SLAVERY
The Anglo-American
Involvement

CHARLOTTE AND DENIS PLIMMER

DAVID & CHARLES: Newton Abbot
BARNES & NOBLE BOOKS: New York
(a division of Harper & Row Publishers, Inc)

This edition first published in 1973
in Great Britain by
David & Charles (Holdings) Limited
Newton Abbot   Devon
in the U.S.A. by
Harper & Row Publishers, Inc.
Barnes & Noble Import Division
0 7153 5955 x *(Great Britain)*
06 495606 7 *(United States)*

Set in 10 on 12pt Plantin by Latimer Trend &
Company Limited Plymouth and printed in Great
Britain by Clarke Doble & Brendon Limited Plymouth

Contents

For
Eva and Leonard Glover

Introduction

Great Britain was not the first of the great slaving nations, nor was the United States the last. Both these dubious distinctions belong to the Arabs, who were buying Africans from other Africans 300 years before Christ, and continued to do so well into our own time.

The transatlantic trade began in 1517, when the first negroes were shipped from West Africa to Spain's American colonies. It engaged, at various periods, ten white nations, and endured until the threshold of the twentieth century. By then an estimated 11 million negroes had been sold by coastal African rulers and marketed in scores of West Indian, North American and South American ports. At least as many more died between capture in Africa and sale in the New World.

Of all the whites who bought, sold or owned slaves, the English and the Americans were the most deeply involved, and their stake was the highest. Slave-trading provided the substructure of England's West Indian sugar economy and of her industrial revolution. In the United States it made possible the cotton and tobacco industries of the South, contributed to the most destructive of all American wars—that between the states—and helped to shape the nation's ethnic composition.

Edmund Ruffin, a nineteenth-century southerner, wrote, 'One of the great benefits of the institution of African slavery to the Southern states is its effect in keeping away from our territory, and directing to the north and northwest, the hordes of immigrants now flowing from Europe.'

Slavery's final legacy, whose ultimate dimensions no man now living can foresee, is the great global division between black and white which bedevils racial harmony, not only in white nations with negro populations, but throughout Africa itself, from the Cape to Cairo, and rubs off on Western–Asian relationships.

The Portuguese, the first Europeans to reach West

Africa, were the innovators and for many years the masters of the trade, supplying their own and Spain's massive colonial labour needs. England's earliest ventures, begun by Sir John Hawkins in 1562, were as much to test the Spanish–Portuguese monopoly in Central America as to indulge in slaving for its own sake. It was not until the beginnings of England's colonisation of the West Indies, early in the seventeenth century, that slaving became a matter of national policy.

Like the Spanish before them, the English soon discovered that the local Indians pined and died under enforced labour. Imported Africans were stronger and more agriculturally orientated, hence better suited to field work on the plantations.

The English perfected the 'triangular trade' pattern which had already been established. Trade goods were shipped from England to Africa to pay for slaves. The slaves were then crammed sardine-tight aboard vessels for the Middle Passage, the long Atlantic crossing to the West Indies, where they were exchanged either for money or for sugar. Back home again, the proceeds paid for a new supply of trade goods. The system reaped handsome profits on all three legs of the journey.

Later, when New Englanders entered the commerce, they evolved a variation of the triangle: buying slaves in Africa with Yankee rum; selling the slaves in the islands for sugar and molasses, and, back in New England, distilling the molasses into more rum with which to buy more slaves.

Slavery, its business requirements and its enormous earnings, interpenetrated the mercantile, military, economic and social patterns of all the white nations which practised it: the Portuguese, the English, the French, the Danes, the Swedes, the Spanish, the Dutch, the Courlanders (a Baltic people), the Brandenburgers and the Americans. The need to control the West African coast, the seas between West Africa and the Americas and the colonial territories where the slaves were employed, caused war after war, either directly or indirectly. The Portuguese fought the Dutch; the Dutch fought the English; the English the Dutch, the French and the slave-voracious Spanish.

Not only did slavery contribute to wars, it also contributed to the ability of slaving nations to wage them. For the trade supported the merchant fleets which in turn furnished trained sailors to the navies of the powers. Nelson was one of many English admirals who saw the slaving ships in this sense as handmaidens to the Royal Navy. It was not until the late eighteenth century that statistics emerged to prove that even more seamen than blacks died of brutality or disease in the Middle Passage, 21·5 per cent as against 12·5 per cent.

On the West African coast the Europeans vied for the favours of the local rulers in whose territories their fortified trading posts or 'factories' stood, and upon whose sufferance and co-operation their livelihoods depended. This was, for the most part, a seller's market, not a buyer's.

The black chieftains controlled the supply of slaves from the hinterland, where few whites dared set foot. They exacted swingeing port duties and demanded royal salutes and other courtly flattery. And they set the price for every negro, bargaining shrewdly, and insisting that the trade goods be in their hands before the slaves were loaded aboard the vessels.

Slaves were produced on demand in a number of ways. If captured during inter-tribal wars, Africans were, by local tradition, legally saleable. So were criminals, and many offences were devised to create a constant 'criminal' supply. If short both of military prisoners and of felons, local kings often simply sacked a town, even in their own nations. Or they ordered fresh stocks to be 'panyared'—kidnapped.

Slaves from the interior were marched, sometimes for hundreds of miles, in long files—'coffles'—

fastened together by chains or thongs. While awaiting purchase they were penned in stockades—'baracoons'. Once paid for, they were branded with the buying company's mark. Across the sea they were re-sold, either aboard ship by 'scramble', in which a flat price was agreed in advance, and buyers grabbed for the strongest and healthiest; or by auction at the dockside. They were then branded anew, this time with the planter's mark. 'Refuse' slaves—those too ill to fetch a reasonable price—were often abandoned on the waterfront to die.

Slaving has been called the most lucrative trade the world has ever known. Its gigantic dividends underwrote the development of the ports of Bristol and Liverpool in England, and of their New England counterparts, Boston and Newport. Later they helped to create entire industrial complexes: railways, docks, coal-mining, iron-smelting. They also financed a vast range of supporting enterprises.

What was good for the slavers of England was good for England herself. When, in the eighteenth century, English abolitionists began to arouse strong anti-slavery sentiments, Parliament was bombarded with petitions demanding protection for the trade. This loose-knit lobby represented not only slave-ship owners and slaving merchants, but also serge-makers, wool-combers, weavers, cutlers, gun-makers, brass- and iron-founders, ship-builders, sail-makers and the manufacturers of chains, locks and manacles.

The same held true for New England, whose businessmen and industrialists, before the break with the Mother Country in 1776, also frequently petitioned Westminster for protection. The English West India lobby operated successfully almost to the end. But the pleas of their North American opposite numbers received less sympathetic hearings.

It seemed to the government that England's willingness to bear the burden of wars which protected the North Americans as well as herself was insufficiently appreciated by the colonial legislatures. The Yankees incurred additional resentment by their growing habit of selling blacks to British planters, demanding payment in bullion rather than produce, and sailing on with their English gold to buy their sugar and molasses cheaper in non-British islands.

The chief losers from these transactions were, of course, the planters. The gainers were primarily the French, secondarily the Dutch. Britain, both to protect her own islanders and to preserve her strategic position in the Caribbean, imposed heavy taxes, as early as 1733, on all produce imported into North America from any other than British possessions.

The Yankee traders fought back: determined to operate their rum distilleries at a profit, they became smugglers. And colonists in general, resenting further taxes and duties imposed by Westminster over the next several decades, riposted by refusing to import taxed goods from Britain or British territories. Taxed tea, of course, ultimately became the most provocative product of all. But the poisoned relations which led to rebellion began with the sugar that sweetened the tea.

In the first hundred years of England's major participation in slavery, the trade's contribution to the imperial exchequer weighed far more heavily in the balance than did the moral scruples of those who abhorred it. Many Quakers, both in England and North America, had traditionally opposed slavery, on the grounds that it contradicted their own humanitarian and religious tenets. And so, indeed, had others.

The philosopher, John Locke, declared in 1689, in his *Treatise on Civil Government*, 'Slavery is so vile and miserable an estate of man, and so directly opposite to the generous temper and courage of our nation, that it is hardly to be conceived that an "Englishman", much less a "gentleman" should plead for it.'

Daniel Defoe, who equated slaving with lechery and drunkenness, wrote in his *Reformation of Manners* (1702):

'The harmless Natives basely they trepan,
And barter Baubles for the *Souls of Men*:
The Wretches they to Christian Climes bring o'er,
To serve worse Heathens than they did before.'

Abolition became a burning issue when men like Granville Sharp, Thomas Clarkson and William Wilberforce banded together, both inside and outside Parliament, to fight against slavery. But before the trade—and later, slave-ownership—could be outlawed, another factor had to be considered: did slaving really pay?

In 1776 the Scots economist, Adam Smith, contended that the colonies were costing England more than they earned. He argued in *The Wealth of Nations*, 'It appears from the experience of all ages and nations that the work done by freemen comes cheaper in the end than that performed by slaves.'

The very availability of slaves, even at high prices, combined with the planters' delusion that they cost no further money out of pocket (except for their miserable food and quarters), bred a kind of spendthrift carelessness. The colonials' work habits and their self-indulgent staff requirements were, by English standards, ludicrous. The household of one typical Jamaica planter included twenty-seven negroes: butlers, coachmen, postilions, seamstresses, cooks, children's nurses and cleaners. Another Jamaican supported 421 field-workers. But at any given time, almost one-third were out of action—ill, too old to work, pregnant or too young.

1 *Boston Harbour: The famous 'tea party' in which Bostonians disguised as Indians threw tea overboard in protest against import taxes. Such imposts were initiated to discourage colonists from buying slave-grown sugar from other than British sources. The duties later spread to other commodities*

2   *Abraham Lincoln debates Stephen A. Douglas (in black) during Illinois senatorial campaign. Poster foreground right pinpoints a major issue: the admission of new territories in the Union as free rather than slave-owning states*

The demise of the triangular trade—that rhythmic workable money machine—could not, it is reasonable to argue, have been achieved without the complicity of the very men who had long stood out against abolition. The Sugar Islands began to lose money! Protected at home by imperial preference, British-grown sugar soon became more costly than that grown by foreigners. English importers clamoured for the freedom to buy it in the most favourable markets, wherever they might be.

The heavily indebted planters had additional problems. The soil in their islands was becoming exhausted. Inexpensive beet sugar, manufactured in England, began to appear even on fashionable tables.

Thanks to a series of wars, the islanders could do virtually no business with Europe. To make matters worse, through those same wars England had gained two new Caribbean possessions, Guiana and Trinidad; if slaved and developed, they could spell crippling competition for the established colonies. In despair, the planters themselves took up the cry to outlaw the trade. Their reasoning: they already owned slaves; if they could prevent the slaving of Guiana and Trinidad, they might yet be saved!

Abolitionists in North America, however, faced more obstacles, not less. Slave labour was increasingly in demand. Virtually the entire South was rural and dependent upon imported human tools. With the invention of the cotton gin in 1793, and the consequent spread of cotton cultivation, the need soared as never before.

Although the concept of owning one's fellow-man was anathema to many of the champions of 'life, liberty and the pursuit of happiness', the make-weight of the southern-plantation aristocracy was too great to brush aside. To oppose it in 1776 would have put the impending emergence of the new nation at risk. Thus, despite the efforts of such men as John Adams, Benjamin Franklin and Thomas Jefferson, the United States entered history as a slave-owning nation. This entailed unforeseen obligations.

When, in the nineteenth century, new slave-owning territories demanded admission into the Union, compromises had to be made. They entered on their own terms—and always with the same rationalisation: the Union must be preserved.

It was to take eighty-nine years from the founding of the nation before the North's victory over the South, and the consequent passage of the thirteenth amendment to the Constitution, brought American slavery to an end.

The last holdouts against abolition in the western hemisphere were Cuba and Brazil, which retained the institution into the 1880s.

CHAPTER ONE

The Making of the Trade (1562-1698)

Sir John Hawkins

Sir John Hawkins was the first English slaver. He made three voyages which foreshadowed the triangular trade that was to come. His initial venture was described by Richard Hakluyt in THE PRINCIPAL NAVIGATIONS *(1589), who wrote from information supplied by Hawkins himself.*

The first voyage of the right worshipfull and valiant knight sir John Hawkins, sometimes treasurer of her Majesties navie Roial, made to the West Indies 1562. Master John Hawkins having made divers voyages to the Iles of the Canaries, and there by his good and upright dealing being growen in love and favour with the people, informed himselfe amongst them by diligent inquisition, of the state of the West India, whereof hee had received some knowledge by the instructions of his father, but increased the same by the advertisements and reports of that people. And being amongst other particulars assured,

that Negros were very good marchandise in Hispaniola, and that store of Negros might easily bee had upon the coast of Guinea, resolved with himselfe to make triall thereof, and communicated that devise with his worshipfull friendes of London: namely with Sir Lionell Ducket, sir Thomas Lodge, M. Gunson his father in law, sir William Winter, M. Bromfield and others. All which persons liked so well of his intention, that they became liberall contributors and adventurers in the action. For which purpose there were three good ships immediately provided: The one called the *Salomon* of the burthern of 120. tunne, wherein M. Hawkins himselfe went as Generall: The second the *Swallow* of 100. tunnes, wherein went for Captaine M. Thomas Hampton: and the third the *Jonas* a barke of 40. tunnes, wherein the Master supplied the Captaines roome: in which small fleete M. Hawkins tooke with him not above 100. men for feare of sicknesse and other inconveniences, whereunto men in long

Qui Vicit totiens in Fructis classibus hostes
Ille magis HAWKINS vitam relliquit in Undis

3 *Sir John Hawkins (1532-95), England's first slaver. He captured 300 blacks in West Africa, sold them to the Spanish in Hispaniola and returned home 'with prosperous successe and much gaine'*

voyages are commonly subject.

With this companie he put off and departed from the coast of England in the moneth of October 1562. and in his course touched first at Teneriffe, where hee received friendly intertainment. From thence he passed to Sierra Leona, upon the coast of Guinea, which place by the people of the countrey is called Tagarin, where he stayed some good time, and got into his possession, partly by the sworde, and partly by other meanes, to the number of 300.

Negros at the least, besides other merchandises which that countrey yeeldeth. With this praye hee sayled over the Ocean sea unto the Iland of Hispaniola, and arrived first at the port of Isabella: and there hee had reasonable utterance of his English commodities, as also of some part of his Negros, trusting the Spaniards no further, than that by his owne strength he was able still to master them. From the port of Isabella he went to Puerto de Plata, where he made like sales, standing alwaies upon his guard: from thence also hee sayled to Monte Cristi another port on the North side of Hispaniola, and the last place of his touching, where he had peaceable traffique, and made vent of the whole number of his Negros: for which he received in those 3. places by way of exchange such quantitie of merchandise, that hee did not onely lade his owne 3. shippes with hides, ginger, sugars, and some quantities of pearles, but he fraighted also two other hulkes with hides and the like commodities, which hee sent into Spaine. And thus leaving the Iland, he returned and disemboqued, passing out by the Ilands of the Caycos, without further entring into the bay of Mexico, in this his first voyage to the West India. And so with prosperous successe and much gaine to himselfe and the aforesayde adventurers, he came home, and arrived in the moneth of September 1563.

At that time, Portugal controlled the West African slave trade, and Spain, her best customer, held a firm grip on the Caribbean. Both nations stigmatised Hawkins's voyages as 'piracy', and the Spanish attacked him at Vera Cruz. This resulted in an inquiry in the High Court of Admiralty. The DEPOSITION OF WILLIAM FOWLER (1569), *a merchant of Ratcliffe, indicates the extent of slave dealing in Spanish America.*

. . . by the experience of the trade w'ch he [Fowler]

hathe had to and at the saide place called Vera Crux and other the cheiffe of the West Indias as is aforesaid this deponent knowethe that a Negro of a good stature and yonge of yeres is worthe and is commonlie bought and soulde there at Mexico and the maine lande of the West Indias for iiiiᶜ vᶜ and viᶜ pesos. For if a negro be a Bossale that is to say ignorant of the spanishe or Portugale tonge then he or she is commonlye soulde for iiiiᶜ and iiiiᶜ L pesos. But if the Negro can speake anye of the foresaide languages any thinge indifferentlye (whiche is called Ladinos) then the same negro is commonlye soulde for vᶜ and viᶜ pesos as the negro is of choise and yonge of yeres And this Deponent seythe that the best trade in those places is of Negros. The trade whereof he this Deponent hathe used and hathe soulde Negros at the saide places and seen other marchantes likewise sell ther Negros there, Divers tymes And thereby knowethe that the common price of negros is as before is Deposed Whiche Negros beinge carried into the Inner and farder partes of the mayne lande of Peru in the west Indias be commonlye sold there for viiiᶜ and ixᶜ pesos.

Slave Labour in the New World

By 1645, British settlers were well established in New World colonies of their own, and increasingly aware of the importance of slaves to their growing economies, both in the West Indies and in North America. George Downing, later Oliver Cromwell's spymaster and the developer of Downing Street, where British prime ministers now live, sent a LETTER *from Barbados to his cousin, John Winthrop Jr, in Massachusetts.*

If you go to Barbados, you shal see a flourishing Iland, many able men. I believe they have bought this year no lesse than a thousand Negroes, and the more they buie, the better able they are to buye, for in a yeare and halfe they will earne (with God's blessing) as much as they cost . . .

4 *Sir George Downing (1623?-84), developer of Downing Street. He spied for both Cromwell and Charles II and applauded the economics of slave-owning. Pepys called him 'a perfidious rogue'*

In the same year, Downing's father, Emanuel, wrote a LETTER *to Winthrop's father, governor of the Massachusetts Bay colony. The two older men were brothers-in-law.*

To his evere-honored brother John Winthrop, Esqr. at Boston.
Sir, . . . If upon a Just warre [with the Indians] the Lord should deliver them into our hands, wee might easily have men woemen and children enough to exchange for Moores, which wilbe more gaynefull pilladge for us than wee conceive, for I doe not see how wee can thrive untill wee get into a stock of

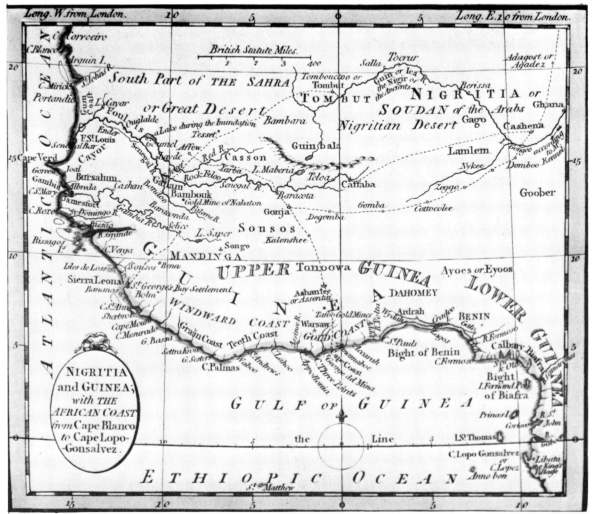

British Statute Miles.

South Part of THE SAHRA

or Great Desert.

TOMBUT

NIGRITIA or SOUDAN of the Arabs

Nigritian Desert

ATLANTIC OCEAN

Cape Verd

Senegal

Gambia

Sierra Leona

GUINEA

MANDINGA

UPPER GUINEA

WINDWARD COAST

Grain Coast

Teeth Coast

GOLD COAST

DAHOMEY

BENIN

Bight of Benin

LOWER GUINEA

Bight of Biafra

GULF OF GUINEA

the Line

ETHIOPIC OCEAN

NIGRITIA and GUINEA; with THE AFRICAN COAST from Cape Blanco to Cape Lopo-Gonsalvez.

5 *West African coast most frequented by European slave-buyers. This bulge was the easiest to reach, and its negroes the most prized. The Gold Coast (now Ghana) was the busiest section of all*

slaves sufficient to doe all our buisiness, for our children's children will hardly see this great Continent filled with people, soe that our servants will still desire freedome to plant for them-selves, and not stay but for verie great wages. And I suppose you know verie well how wee shall mayneteyne 20 Moores cheaper than one Englishe servant.

The ships that shall bring Moores may come home laden with salt which may beare most of the chardge, if not all of it ...

Although the British did not organise slaving on a

substantial scale until after the restoration of Charles II, there were earlier sporadic attempts to structure a system of trade with West Africa. The operations of the Guinea Company, typified in the following LETTER OF INSTRUCTIONS *to a ship's captain (1651), anticipated those of two bodies later to operate under royal charter, the Company of Royal Adventurers of England Trading into Africa, and the Royal African Company.*

London, the 9 of December, 1651. *Mr. Bartholomewe Haward,* First we pray you performe your dayly dutie unto Almightie God, that so we may expect a blessing upon your endeavours.

You are to hasten with your ship to Gravesend, and being cleered there into the Downes, and from thence with the first faire winde and weather, in Compa. with such ships as you shall finde, to saile directlie for the River Gambra in Guinny, where you shall finde the ship *Freindship* Capt. Jno. Blake Comaunder, upon w'ch ship Mr. James Pope is our cheif factor, to whome you are to deliver our Letter, and such Cargo as we have laden in you (excepting the cases of sugar chest boards belonging unto Mr. John Wood) unto whome we have written to buy and put aboard you so many negers as yo'r ship can cary, and for what shalbe wanting to supply with Cattel, as also to furnish you with victualls and provisions for the said negers and Cattel, as also with such Caske as Capt. Blake can spare, to be filled with water, all w'ch we have desired Mr. Pope to effect in as short a time as may be, and when he shall have laden your Cargo of negers or Cattel aboard, you are to signe bills of ladeing for what you shall receive desireing his letter to Mr. Francis Soane Mercht at Barbados unto whome we have written effectually for the sale of your negers, and ladeing your ship for London, whose order and directions you are to followe untill he shall give you your dispatch for London. Wee desire you to be veary carefull in the well stoweing of your ship and that none of the goods you shall take aboard be abused, and being dispatched from thence we pray you hasten for London, and when you come int our Chanell be veary vigilant and carefull for feare of surprysalls, not trusting any. And our ord'r is that all the while you lye in the River Gambra untill your Cargo be provided that you followe the directions of Mr. James Pope and from all places where you shall touch send us advice of your proceedings. There is put aboard your Pinck *Supply* 30 paire of shackles and boults for such of your negers as are rebellious and we pray you be veary carefull to keep them under and let them have their food in due season that they ryse not against you, as they have done in other ships.

When you shall come into the Downes you are to send unto Mr. Thomas Waad at Dover for a case of Cristall beads w'ch he will put aboard you there w'ch you are to cary with you for Gambra and deliver with the rest of the Cargo unto Mr. James Pope. So Comitting you to God's protection we rest Your loving freinds.

ROW: WILSON
THOMAS WALTER
THO: CHAMBRELAN
JOHN WOODS
MAURICE THOMSON

There were occasional instances of consideration for the negro even in the early days. One of the first acts that tried to ensure emancipation for slaves in North America was passed by the General Court of Election at Warwick, Rhode Island, on 19 May 1652. There is no record, however, of this ACT'S *ever having been enforced.*

Whereas, there is a common course practised amongst English men to buy negers, to that end they may have them for service or slaves forever; for the preventinge of such practises among us, let it be ordered, that no blacke mankind or white being forced by covenant bond, or otherwise, to serve any man or his assignes longer than ten yeares, or untill they come to bee twentie four yeares of age, if they bee taken in under fourteen, from the time of their cominge within the liberties of this Collonie. And at the end or terme of ten yeares to sett them free, as the manner is with the English servants. And that man that will not let them goe free, or shall sell them away elsewhere, to that end that they may bee enslaved to others for a long time, hee or they shall forfeit to the Collonie forty pounds.

Earlier that same year, the directors of the DUTCH WEST INDIA COMPANY, *whose nation then led the world's slave trade, had written to the thriving Netherlands colony 'at the Manhattans'.*

And in order that you may be the more fully assured of our good intention, we do hereby consent that the commonalty yonder shall have liberty to repair to the coast of Angola and Africa, and transport thence as many negroes as they will make use of for the cultivation of their lands, on the conditions and regulations which are sent herewith to the Director.

Amsterdam, 4th April, 1652.

Company of Royal Adventurers
English efforts to trade for slaves were frequently frustrated by the aggressive Dutch. King Charles II, in establishing his Company of Royal Adventurers, had served notice upon them and other rivals that slavery was now a major English concern. The new company's secretary established TERMS FOR SLAVE-SUPPLY *to the West Indies in a letter (1662) to Francis Lord Willoughby, chief governor of England's Caribbean colonies.*

My Lord, the Royal Company being very sensible how necessary it is that the English Plantations in America should have a competent and a constant

6 *King Charles II (1630-85), the first to structure the English trade. He chartered two successive monopolies, but foreign competition and English interlopers forced them out of business*

supply of Negro-servants for their own use of Planting, and that at a moderate Rate, have already sent abroad, and shall within eight days dispatch so many Ships for the Coast of Africa as shall by Gods permission furnish the said Plantations with at least 3000 Negroes, and will proceed from time to time to provide them a constant and sufficient succession of them, so as the Planter shall have no just cause to complain of any Want: And for the Price, and terms of Payment, they have for the present resolved, to order all their Servants and Factors not to sell any Negroes higher than is expressed in this following Resolve.

Resolved, That Orders be given to the Factors in the Plantations of the Charibee Islands, to sell all Blacks that are found in Lotts (as hath been customary) at £17. sterling p. head in Money (ps. of 8/8 Sivil and Mexico at 4 sh.) or Bills Exchange for England with good assurance of payment, or at 2400 *l*. of well cured Muscovado Sugar in Cask, with express condition, that no Blacks be delivered without present payment in Money, Bills, or Sugar, viewed and accepted by the Factors, or in Cotton or Indico, according to the price currant between them and Sugar.

And do desire your Lordship . . . to gather from the Planters and Inhabitants, and to transmit to us as soon as they conveniently can, the certain number of Negroes which they desire, and will engage to receive yearly from Us on those reasonable Terms proposed, that so we may proportion our Care for them accordingly . . .

By Order of the Royal Company:
ELLIS LEIGHTON, SECRET.

Two days later he offered shares in the organisation to English investors. DECLARATION OF THE COMPANY OF ROYAL ADVENTURERS:

To all His Majesties Native Subjects in General: the Publique Declaration and Invitation of the Company of Royal Adventurers of England Trading into Africa. Whereas the Kings most Excellent Majesty hath seriously considered what Profit and Honour did formerly accrew to His good Subjects by the Trade of Africa . . . and His Majesty finding that . . . by reason of the universal intestine Confusion of the Times . . . other Nations have taken confidence so far to invade and disturb His Majesties Subjects in the said Trade, that it is in danger utterly to be lost to this Nation, and thereby His Majesties Dominions in America in apparent hazard to be rendered useless in their growing Plantations, through want of that usual supply of Servants which they have hitherto

7 *A device to stop a captive from escaping in the African jungle: the hooks would entangle him in the vegetation. Also used as a punishment in the West Indies to prevent his lying down and sleeping*

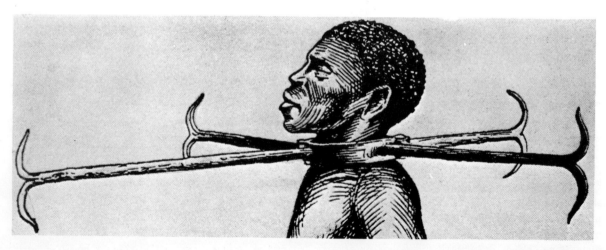

had from Africa; which mischief cannot be prevented but by His Majesties Re-establishing the said Trade, and erecting a Corporation under the special Protection of His Royal Authority, consisting of such persons of Honour and Experience, as may by a considerable Joynt-Stock, and Common Counsel, vigorously assert the Right thereof.

And His Majesty having to that end been graciously pleased to grant to His Royal Highness the Duke of York, and others, (who have already formed and employed a Joynt-Stock of seventeen thousand and four hundred pounds) His Letters Patents for the Incorporation and Regulation of the whole Trade of Africa from Cape Blanc to Cape de bona Esperanza: His Royal Highness therefore, and the rest of the Royal Company, desiring to communicate the advantage of the said Trade to all His Majesties Subjects in general, thought fit to give notice, and do hereby give notice, and publish to all His Majesties native Subjects of England;

That all or any of them that live within the City of London, or twenty miles thereabouts, may at any time before the twentieth day of October next ensuing the date hereof, and those that live in other parts of the Kingdom before the fifth of November following, freely be admitted into the said Corporation and Joynt-Stock, subscribing at least four hundred pounds respectively . . .

Dutch Reprisals
The Dutch struck back quickly. And the company warned the king of further trouble to come in this REPORT *(1663):*

. . . the Dutch have endeavoured to drive the English Company from the coast, have followed their ships from port to port, and hindered them coming nigh the shore to trade; they have persuaded the negroes to destroy their servants and to take their forts, have seized their boats and goods, violently taken possession of Cape Coast, and shot at his Majesty's Royal flag . . . had it not been for the countenance of some of his Majesty's ships, to give the Company a respect in the eyes of the natives and preserve their forts, the Company had ere this been stripped of their possessions and interests in Africa; Cormantin Castle itself being in extreme danger when the *Marmaduke* and *Speedwell* arrived there. The Dutch . . . say they will force the English from their forts if they do not quit them.

The Royal African Company
The company's fears were justified. The Dutch fleet scized all but one of their trading posts, and by 1667 the Adventurers had collapsed with a loss of over £120,000. In 1672 the resilient king chartered a new monopoly, the Royal African Company. Two years later, in the light of competition not only from foreign slavers but from interloping British skippers, he made a PROCLAMATION.

. . . We have thought fit, with Advice of Our Privy Council, to Publish and Declare Our Royal Will and Pleasure to be, And We do hereby strictly Prohibit and Forbid all and every of Our Subjects whatsoever, Except the said Royal Company and their Successours, at any time or times hereafter, to send or Navigate any Ship or Ships, Vessel or Vessels, or Exercise any Trade from any of Our Plantations, Dominions, or Countreys in America, to any of the Parts or Coasts of Africa . . . to carry any Negro Servants, Gold, Elephants Teeth, or any other Goods or Merchandizes of the Product or Manufacture of the said Places, to any of Our American Dominions or Plantations, upon pain of Our high Displeasure, and the forfeiture and loss of the said Negro's, Gold, Elephants Teeth, and all other Goods and Merchandizes, and the Ship or Vessels which shall bring or carry the same . . .

Given at Our Court at Whitehall, the Thirtieth

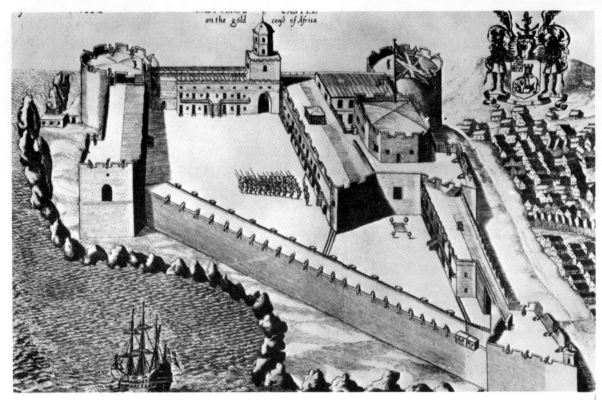

8, 9 *Cape Coast Castle, Ghana, a trading fort built by the Swedes in 1655 and, soon after, acquired and enlarged by the British. Such castles housed slaving officials, troops and artisans, and had stockades for slaves awaiting sale. (Opposite) The castle is today a museum of West African history*

day of November, in the Six and twentieth year of Our Reign.

God save the King.

Trading for Slaves

Trading for slaves was arduous, painstaking and often discouraging. Captain Robert Doegood, master of the Royal African Company's ship Arthur, *described transactions in his* LOG (*1678*).

. . . *Munday 11 February* [1678]. This day aboutt nine in the morninge Came one Board the Kinge of New Calabarr with some others of his gen'tes and after a Long discourse Came to Agreem'tt for Currentt for negro man 36 Copper Barrs: for on[e] negro woman 30 and for one monello [metal ring used in trading] eight yames . . .

Wednesday 13 February [1678]. The 12th day wee bought 3 men 3 women as your hon'rs will finde one my Books of Acc'tt and this day wee Bo 14 men and 18 women very good and young negroes with some provisions for them . . .

Fryday 8 [March 1678]. This day wee Bought 2 men and 1 woman haveinge nott many Cannows one Board to take greater Choice therfore did forbare to

purchase expecting more for to Chuse for your hon'rs Better advantage Resolvinge as was befor minded to Buye not any Butt such as might If Life might bee permitted Answer your hon'rs expectation and advantage:

The 7 day aboutt four in the afternoon died one woman. This day as will appeare y're accompt wee did nott purchase any Negroes Butt some provisions for negroes: wee have many sick Captives Butt take the greatest Care wee can to preserve . . .

Munday 22 [April 1678. At sea]. This day the winde nott Blowinge soe Fresh I did Muster the Negroes Causeing all to goe Downe Between decks that were weell and soe counted them up giveinge as they Came up one after one, Beinge all out of Sheckells, Tobacco: and found to be alife 155 men 119 women 9 Boyes 9 Girles and noe more, this afternoone died one woman . . .

Tuesday 28 [May 1678. Barbados]. This day were many of your hon'rs Negroes sold . . .

31 [May 1678]. The next day Rainy weather were not many Buyers one Board: if itt had been Fare Weather suppose had sold all the Negroes—there were 23 Left unsold: and the next day Beinge Satterday Mr. man Came on Board By your hon'rs Agentts order and Caused them to be Caryed away. I suppose the were sold: after the negroes were all outt I Left the shipp and went one shore . . .

10, 11 *Christiansborg Castle, Ghana, built in the 1660s by the Danes who bought the site from the Paramount Chief of Accra for 100oz of gold. The British took over in 1850, and the castle flew the Union Jack as residence of governors general of the Gold Coast* (opposite) *until Ghana's independence. It now houses Ghanaian heads of state*

The Factors in Africa

The mortality of slaves runs like a threnody through the trade's history. They died of melancholy, of disease, of torture, of the sheer impossibility of living on the stifling slave decks of the Middle Passage. A MEMORANDUM FROM THE FACTORS *at Cape Coast Castle to the company (1681):*

In answer to what your Honours are pleased to suggest concerning Capt. Woodfin's Negroes whereof 160 died and no complaint made of their Goodness wee are apt to beleive that had he taken in only 400 there had few miscarried and wee find that the Covetousness of Command'rs Crowding in their Slaves above their proportion for the advantage of Freight is the only reason of the great Loss to the Compa. If your Honours would be pleased to beate them down in their number though you gave them five shillings per head exterordinary Your Honours would be considerable gainers at the yeares end.

The same factors objected to unsaleable trade merchandise:

Wee are Sorry wee must complaine of our late deed trading att Cabo Corse occasioned by the want of

goods we wrot your Honours for and it grived us the more to see our Neighbours att the Mine [the Dutch at Elmina Castle] . . . take great Pride to shew the English how well they are furnished with all sorts of goods and how their ware houses are cramed with Prodigious quantitys . . .

Wee have added a Cattalogue of goods most vendible at this Place which by all opertunityes wee fail not to acquaint your Honours there being some small additions to what was in our last *vizt.* 500 P's Saies [type of serge], 1500 P's Perpetuanoes [English woollen cloth] (800 of which must be green, 600 blew and 100 red) but not any Printed for they will not sell Lett the collours be what they will . . . 600 Brawles [striped Indian cloth], 5 Callicoe Clouts, 500 one pound Pewt'r Basons, 150 2 lb. Ditto, 150

3 lb. Ditto, 150 4 lb. Ditto . . . 100 Ginghams, the Red Stript best, 5000 Sheetes, 600 broad Tapseiles [Indian cotton], 300 Narrow ditto, 500 Long Clothes white, 100 half firk's Tallow, 100 Dozen Knives ordinary . . . Without your Honors are pleased to supply us with . . . good store . . . you will un-avoidably Lose considerably by those Ships you send to take their Slaves in here upon the Gold Coast what for the greate scarcity of them and the extravagant pizes [prices] that are given by the com-manders of ships.

Planters Oppose the Company

Complaints against the company came from many sources, in particular from the planters it had been founded to serve. One group in Barbados produced a bill of particulars, THE GROANS OF THE PLANTATIONS *(1689):*

HERETOFORE we might send to *Guiney* for *Negroes* when we wanted them. and they stood us in about seven pound a Head. The Account is short and plain. For they cost the value of forty shillings a Head in *Guiney*; and their freight was five pound, for every one that was brought alive, and could go over the Ship side. But now we are shut out of this Trade: and a Company is put upon us, from whom we must have our *Negroes*, and no other way. A Com-pany of London Merchants have got a Patent, ex-cluding all others, to furnish the Plantations with *Negroes*: some great Men being joyned with them, with whom we were not able to contend. But those great Men might have had some better Exercise for their Generosity, than the pressing too hard upon (we must not say, oppressing) industrious People. And now we buy *Negroes* at the price of an Engross'd Commodity: the common Rate of a good *Negro* on Ship board being twenty pound. And we are forced to scramble for them in so shameful a Manner, that one of the great Burdens of our Lives is the going to buy *Negroes* . . .

There never want fair Pretences for the foulest Monopolies. But what do they pretend for this? They will tell you that (to the common Good and Benefit of the *English* Nation) they can deal with the People of *Africa* to much better advantage, by being a Company. And so they might, if they could shut out other Nations. But since the *Dutch, French, Danes, Swedes* and others, trade thither . . . they can shut out none but the poor *English* . . . And it plainly appears, that 'tis not upon the People of *Africa,* but upon the *English* Planters in *America,* that they make their advantage . . .

12 *A sugar-crushing plant run by waterpower. So important was cane to England's Caribbean possessions that they became known as 'the Sugar Islands'. Slaves were the planters' entire work force.*

Of all the Things we have occasion for, *Negroes* are the most necessary, and the most valuable. And therefore to have them under a Company, and under a Monopoly, whereby their prices are more than doubled, nay almost trebled; cannot but be most grievous to us. Many an Estate hath been sunk and many a Family hath been ruin'd, by the high prices they give for *Negroes* . . .

Our Negroes, which cost us so dear, are also extremely casual. When a man hath bought a parcel of the best and ablest he can get for money; let him take all the care he can, he shall lose a full third part of them, before they ever come to do him service. When they are season'd, and used to the Country, they stand much better. but to how many Mischances are the[y] still subject? If a Stiller slip into

a Rum-Cistern, it is sudden death: for it stifles in a moment. If a Mill-feeder be catch't by the finger, his whole body is drawn in, and he is squeez'd to pieces. If a Boyler get any part into the scalding Sugar, it sticks like Glew or Birdlime, and 'tis hard to save either Limb or Life. They will quarrell, and kill one another, upon small occasions: by many Accidents they are disabled, and become a burden: they will run away, and perhaps never be seen more: or they will hang themselves, no creature knows why. And sometimes there comes a Mortality amongst them, which sweeps a great part of them away.

When this happens, the poor Planter is in a hard condition: especially if he be still indebted for them. He must have more Negroes or his Works must stand, and he must be ruin'd at once. And he cannot procure them without contracting new Debts; which perhaps he shall never be able to work out . . .

Log of a Slaver

One of the most vivid pictures of seventeenth-century slaving comes down to us from the JOURNAL OF THOMAS PHILLIPS (*1694*), *commander of the company's ship* Hannibal, *450 tons, 36 guns.*

. . . *May the 19th.* Steering along shore within three leagues, with fine easy gale, we spy'd a canoe making off towards us, whereupon we lay by and staid for her; when she came aboard the master of her brought in three women and four children to sell, but they ask'd very dear for them, and they were almost dead for want of victuals, looking like meer skeletons, and so weak that they could not stand, so that they were not worth buying . . . we were upon the Alampo coast, which negroes are esteem'd the worst and most washy of any that are brought to the West-Indies, and yield the least price; why I know not, for they seem as well limb'd and lusty as any other negroes, and the only difference I perceiv'd in them, was, that they are not so black as the others,

and are all circumcis'd, which no negroes else upon the whole coast (as I observ'd) are: The negroes most in demand at Barbadoes, are the gold coast, or, as they call them, Cormantines, which will yield 3 or 4 *l.* a head more than the Whidaws, or, as they call them, Papa negroes; but these are preferr'd before the Angola, as they are before the Alampo, which are accounted the worst of all . . .

May the 21st . . . Our factory [at Whydah] lies about three miles from the sea-side . . . [It] stands low near the marshes, which renders it a very unhealthy place to live in; the white men the African company send there, seldom return to tell their tale: 'tis compass'd round with a mud-wall, about six foot high, and on the south-side is the gate; within is a large yard, a mud thatch'd house, where the factor lives, with the white men; also a store-house, a trunk for slaves, and a place where they bury their dead white men, call'd, very improperly, the hog-yard . . .

The factor, Mr. Peirson, was a brisk man, and had good interest with the king, and credit with the subjects, who knowing their tempers, which is very dastard, had good skill in treating them both civil and rough, as occasion requir'd . . .

As soon as the king understood of our landing, he sent two of his cappasheirs, or noblemen, to compliment us at our factory, where we design'd to continue, that night, and pay our devoirs to his majesty next day, which we signify'd to them, and they, by a foot-express, to their monarch; whereupon he sent two more of his grandees to invite us there that night, saying he waited for us, and that all former captains used to attend him the first night: whereupon being unwilling to infringe the custom, or give his majesty any offence, we . . . were carry'd to the king's town . . .

We returned him thanks by his interpreter, and assur'd him how great affection our masters, the royal African company of England, bore to him, for his civility and fair and just dealings with their captains; and that notwithstanding there were many other places, more plenty of negro slaves that begg'd their custom, yet they had rejected all the advantageous offers made them out of their good will to him, and therefore had sent us to trade with him, to supply his country with necessaries, and that we hop'd he would endeavour to continue their favour by his kind usage and fair dealing with us in our trade, that we may have our slaves with all expedition, which was the making of our voyage; that he would oblige his cappasheirs to do us justice, and not impose upon us in their prices; all which we should faithfully relate to our masters, the royal African company, when we came to England. He answer'd that the African company was a very good brave man; that he lov'd him; that we should be fairly dealt with, and not impos'd upon . . . so after having examin'd us about our cargoe, what sort of goods we had, and what quantity of slaves we wanted, etc., we took our leaves and return'd to the factory, having promised to come in the morning to make our palavera, or agreement, with him about prices, how much of each of our goods for a slave.

. . . he and his cappasheirs exacted very high, but at length we concluded . . . then the bell was order'd to go about to give notice to all people to bring their slaves to the trunk to sell us . . .

When we were at the trunk, the king's slaves, if he had any, were the first offer'd to sale, which the cappasheirs would be very urgent with us to buy, and would in a manner force us to it ere they would shew us any other, saying they were the Reys Cosa [king's property], and we must not refuse them, tho' as I observ'd they were generally the worst slaves in the trunk, and we paid more for them than any others, which we could not remedy, it being one of his majesty's prerogatives: then the cappasheirs each brought out his slaves according to his degree and quality, the greatest first, etc. and our surgeon

examin'd them well in all kinds, to see that they were sound wind and limb, making them jump, stretch out their arms swiftly, looking in their mouths to judge of their age; for the cappasheirs are so cunning, that they shave them all close before we see them, so that let them be never so old we can see no grey hairs in their heads or beards; and then having liquor'd them well and sleek with palm oil, 'tis no easy matter to know an old one from a middle-age one, but by the teeths decay; but our greatest care of all is to buy none that are pox'd, lest they should infect the rest aboard . . .

. . . we mark'd the slaves we had bought in the breast, or shoulder, with a hot iron, having the letter of the ship's name on it, the place being before anointed with a little palm oil, which caus'd but little pain, the mark being usually well in four or five days, appearing very plain and white after . . .

The negroes are so wilful and loth to leave their own country, that they have often leap'd out of the canoes, boat and ship, into the sea, and kept under water till they were drowned, to avoid being taken up and saved by our boats, which pursued them; they having a more dreadful apprehension of Barbadoes than we can of hell, tho' in reality they live much better there than in their own country; but home is home, etc: we have likewise seen divers of them eaten by the sharks, of which a prodigious number kept about the ships in this place, and I have been told will follow her hence to Barbadoes, for the dead negroes that are thrown over-board in the passage . . .

We had about 12 negroes did wilfully drown themselves, and others starv'd themselves to death; for 'tis their belief that when they die they return home to their own country and friends again . . .

The End of the Slaving Monopoly
Like most government-sponsored monopolies, the Royal African Company bred its own opposition. More and

13 *British naval officers attend a levee of the King of Dahomey. Relationships with African rulers involved flattery as well as shrewdness, from the start to the end of the trade*

more, freebooting interlopers defied the royal displeasure (by now, that of William III); and hardpressed planters bought cut-price blacks whenever they could. To this irresistible force, company and government eventually yielded, and slavery's outlaws became the company's in-laws by ACT OF PARLIAMENT (*9 and 10 Wm III, c 26*), *1698.*

II. . . . Be it further enacted That it shall and may be lawfull to and for any of the Subjects of His Majesties Realm of England as well as for the [Royal African] Company from and after the said Four and twentieth Day of June to trade from England, and from and after the First of August One thousand six hundred ninety and eight from any of His Majesties Plantations and Colonies in America, to and for the Coast of Africa between Cape Mount and the Cape of Good Hope, the said Company and all other the said Subjects answering and paying for the Uses [of the company's shore facilities and for military protection] a Duty of Ten Pounds per Centum ad Valorem for the Goods and Merchandize to be exported from England or from any of His Majesties Plantations or Colonies . . .

CHAPTER TWO

The Working of the Trade (1704-35)

The Ten-per-centers

The legalised ten-per-centers proved both shrewd and avaricious, forcing the Royal African Company to fight hard for its share of the market. This LETTER to the company from Sir Dalby Thomas, governor of Cape Coast Castle, in what is now Ghana, illuminates the intense rivalry.

CAPE COAST CASTLE, 14 Jan. 1704.
The *Rooke*-galley, and your *Davers*-galley, are still at Annamaboe, purchasing their slaves, and as yet met but with very indifferent success, the first having purchased only 60, and the latter 28 Negroes. The 10 per cent. men who are there, spoil the markets extremely, by out-bidding us all at once, by which means they began to out-do your ships in buying, until that I, being advised thereof, ordered your factors and captains to give as much for a Negro, and sell your goods as cheap as they; for I am resolved not to hold the candle to them any longer, as was

done by my predecessors, let the consequence be as it will. You have been sufferers in the trade enough by that already, and since one or other must unavoidably be done, I think that buying and selling at or near their price is the better of the two; for, considering the expence you are at upon the coast, it is better to trade at any rate, than not at all . . .

The Economics of Slavery

Colonists were by no means unanimous about slave-ownership. Although the New Englanders were to become the greatest American slavers, they had small need of blacks for their own use: their farms were compact compared with the sprawling southern plantations. Moreover, their severe winters made survival for the jungle-bred Africans difficult. In any case, the whites did not trust the loyalty of the blacks. No moral issue was involved, but hard-headed practicality, as the Boston NEWS LETTER of 10 June 1706 makes clear:

14 *African dealers selling slaves to whites on the Guinea coast. The recumbent negro* (centre) *is being examined by a purchaser. The woman* (left centre) *has been bought and is being branded*

By last Years Bill of Mortality for the Town of Boston in Numb 100 *News Letter*, we are furnished with a List of 44 Negroes dead last year, which being computed one with another at 30 *l:* per Head, amounts to the Sum of One Thousand three hundred and Twenty Pounds, of which we would make this Remark: That the Importing of Negroes into this or the Neighbouring Provinces is not so beneficial either to the Crown or Country, as White Servants would be.

For Negroes do not carry Arms to defend the Country as Whites do:

Negroes are generaly Eye-Servants, great Thieves, much addicted to stealing, Lying and Purloining.

They do not People our Country as Whites would do whereby we should be strengthened against an Enemy.

By Encouraging the importing of White Men Servants, allowing somewhat to the importer, most Husbandmen in the Country might be furnished with Servants for 8, 9 or 10 *l.* a Head, who are not able to launch out 40 or 50 *l.* for a Negro the now common Price . . .

Were Merchants and Masters Encouraged as

already said to bring in Men Servants, there needed not be such complaint against Superiors Impressing our Children to the War [against the French and their allies, the Indians], there would then be Men enough to be had without Impressing.

The bringing in of such servants would much enrich this Province, because Husbandmen would not only be able far better to manure what Lands are already under Improvement, but would also improve a great deal more that now lyes waste under Woods, and enable this Province to set about raising of Naval Stores, which would be greatly advantagious to the Crown of England, and this Province ...

Suppose the Government here should allow Forty Shillings per head for five years, to such as should Import every of those years 100 White Men Servants, and each to serve 4 Years, the cost would be but 200 *l.* a year, and a 1000 for the five years: the first 100 servants being free the 4th year, they serve the 5th for Wages, and the 6th there is 100 that goes out into the Woods, and settles a 100 Families to strengthen and Baracade us from the Indians, and so a 100 Families more every year successively ...

Not only was the company itself in trouble, but so were the merchants and manufacturers who supplied its trade goods and maritime equipment. The economy of slaving had already interpenetrated the economy as a whole. PETITIONS *from dyers, packers, shipwrights, sail-makers, weavers, iron-workers and tuckers, among others, poured into the Commons.*

January 28, 1709.
A Petition of the Gun-makers, Cutlers and Powder-makers, inhabiting in and about the City of London, was presented to the House, and read; setting forth, that the Petitioners, and their Families, have been very much supported by Sale of their Goods, usually exported by the Royal African Company; which Trade, from the late great Difficulties the Company have met with under the present Settlement, has very much declined, and is in danger of being lost to the Nation, to the Prejudice of the Publick, and utter Ruin of many of the Petitioners: And praying, that the Traffick of the Royal African Company to Africa may be preserved, and encouraged, by such means, as the House shall think fit.

The Asiento
The biggest prize in the international slave trade was the Asiento, *a contract granted by the Crown of Spain which gave to the licensee the sole right to ship negroes to Spain's New World possessions: Central America, Florida, most of South America and many of the Caribbean islands.*

At first the Asiento *went to individual merchants, later to whichever nation held maritime supremacy. England won it in 1713 under the Treaty of Utrecht which ended the War of the Spanish Succession and established her as Europe's leading commercial power, with control over the West African coast from the Gambia River to the Congo. The South Sea Company (founded 1711) contracted, in co-operation with the Royal African Company, to supply Spanish America with 144,000 slaves over thirty years, in return for which they paid King Philip V a flat sum of 200,000 crowns, plus $33\frac{1}{3}$ crowns for every slave delivered. They also paid one quarter of their profits to the Spanish treasury, and a second quarter to the English.*

South Sea Company's ships which picked up negroes from the Royal African Company's forts carried STATEMENTS OF AUTHORISATION.

Wednesday the 4th Nov. 1713.
Be it known unto all men to whom these presents shall come that Capt. Peter Solgard Com'dr of the Ship *St. Mark* burthen 180 Tunns or thereabouts

15 *Throughout the eighteenth century, wars bedevilled England, her colonies and the trade. A hit-and-run enemy raid could cripple a lonely island's economy*

To the Honourable

The Commons in Parliament

ASSEMBLED.

The CASE *of the Poor distressed Planters, and other Inhabitants of the Islands of* Nevis, *and St.* Christophers, *in A-merica.*

THE *French,* in *February* and *March,* 170⁴⁄₅, landed on those Islands, and Burnt and Destroyed almost all the Dwelling-Houses, Sugar-Works, and other Buildings, carried away the greatest part of the Negroes, Coppers, Stills, Merchandizes, and other valuable Goods, to the real Damage of the Inhabitants and Traders, *Five Hundred Thousand Pounds Sterling,* and *upwards.*

The Inhabitants are thereby reduced to the greatest Extremity, having no Houses to dwell in, but what are rais'd with Wild-Canes, which cannot shelter them from the Injuries of the Weather, (very pernicious in those Parts.)

And therefore the Honourable House of Commons, in 170⁶⁄₇, were pleas'd, in Compassion to the distressed Inhabitants to address her Majesty in their Behalf.

Whereupon her Majesty was graciously pleased to appoint Commissioners in those Islands, to compute their Losses, taken upon Oath, the Amount of which, return'd to her Majesty, appears to be *Three Hundred Fifty Six Thousand Nine Hundred Twenty Six Pounds, Ten Shillings and a Penny,* which the *Poor Sufferers* hope this Honourable House will take into their Consideration.

This Kingdom loses yearly, during their present deplorable Condition, at least *a Hundred and Fifty Thousand Pound Sterling;* for, whereas, before the Calamity, they sent Home *Twelve Thousand* Hogsheads of Sugar yearly, now they cannot exceed *Two Thousand,* besides the Loss, by not exporting such large Quantities of the Manufactures of this Kingdom.

They are now in want of Negroes, Mills, Stills, Coppers, and all sorts of Iron-Ware, besides necessary Clothing, which they have always had from Hence, and must have, when in a Condition to procure them.

The Inhabitants of the said Islands, consisting of many Hundred Families of very Diligent and Useful People, have, since that great Calamity, been able to do little more than Plant themselves Provisions, yet have hitherto been persuaded to continue on the Islands, thro' the Comfortable Hopes of a seasonable Relief; but should the People Desert those Islands, the *French* would soon settle them, which would make *them* so powerful in those Parts, as would endanger not only the Loss of the other Leward Islands, but also the whole Sugar Trade of those Parts, with all its Advantages; together with the Imployment of so many Ships yearly.

'Tis therefore Humbly hoped, this Honourable House will compleat and bring to Perfection, so beneficial a Charity, and enable the Inhabitants to Resettle those Islands, that their Families may be preserved from Ruine, and the Revenues of the Crown Augmented.

16 *William Penn (1644-1718), founder of Pennsylvania, signs a peace treaty with the Indians. Though a Quaker, he owned slaves. Many other Quakers traded in or profited from blacks until the late 1700s*

manned with the Said Com'dr. and 25 Men is freighted by us the English Company of the Assiento to Saile from London to the Coast of Africa and from thence with 280 Negros or thereabouts to proceed, for Carthagena or any other the Ports of the Spanish Domin's on the North Side of America pursuant to the Contract made between the Queen of Great Brittain and His Catholick Maj'ty signd at Madrid the 26th March 1713 for carrying on the Assiento trade for the furnishing Negros to the Spanish West Indies. Wherefore wee recomend him the said Capt. Com'dr Capt. Solgard or his Successor, his Ship, the *St. Mark*, all his men, and the said

280 Negros, or so many of them as shall be living at his Arrival in any of the said Ports and during his Stay there to protection of the Generalls and Governours of his said Catholick Maj't and to request from them the admission of the aforesaid Negros for Sale according to the Articles of the Assiento aforemencon'd, for truth whereof we have here to affix the Seal of the Said Company.

Slave Sale

Slavery stirred few Christian consciences. But questioning voices were heard among the Quakers of North America, even though many were slave-owners and, some, slaving skippers. As early as 1688 there had been indications of the lead they were later to take in the fight for abolition. At a meeting in Germantown, Pennsylvania, they had observed: 'Tho' they are black, we cannot conceive there is more liberty to have them as slaves as it is to have other white ones . . . Those who steal or robb men and those who buy or purchase them, are they not all alike?'

Such soft speaking by gentle voices did nothing to deter the traders. A typical ADVERTISEMENT *in New-port, Rhode Island, presaged that city's emergence as the premier port for Yankee slavers.*

NEW-PORT, RHODE-ISLAND, JUNE 2d, 1721. By Order of the Court of Admiralty, There are Nineteen Negroes whereof Two are Men, Eleven Women, Four Boyes and Two Girls, to be Exposed to Sale by Publick Vendue on Wednesday the Fourteenth Day of this Instant June, at Two of the Clock in the Afternoon, at the Town School-House . . . Where all Persons that are inclined to buy the said Negroes, Cocoa or Sugars; or any one of the said Negroes, or part or parcel of said Cocoa or Sugars, are hereby invited to resort. The Conditions of Sale to be seen at the Coffee House, and at the Register's Office, both in the said New Port at any Convenient Hours Three Days preceding the time of Sale.

That same year, the Royal African Company, spurred by both foreign and domestic competition, inaugurated what today we would call a programme of market research. A committee DIRECTIVE *advised:*

. . . a Thorough knowledge of the Inland parts of Africa may prove of very great advantage to the Company . . . Your Agents have Orders as often as any parcells of Negros are brought down to be sold, to make as Strict an Enquiry as possible to find out what Sort of Country they came from . . .

How many days they have employed in their March down from their own Country, whereby its distance from the Forts may be pretty near guessed at?

Whether they have any large or Navigable Rivers in it?

What form of Government they have? and in what manner Justice is exercised? Whether they are guided by any Written Laws, or Customs, or Absolutely by the Will of their Prince?

Of what Extent their Country is? What manner o Citys they have? How large and of what Materials they are built? and of what distance, and how many days journey they are situated from the Neighbouring Nations? as also what sort of people those Neighbouring Nations are?

How populous they are? or how many fighting Men their Armys generally Speaking Consist of?

Their manner of making Slaves? Whether they become so by any other misfortune than that of being taken Prisoners in War time? And whether they have any other method of Trading for them than this of bringing them down to the Coast of Africa to sell to the Europeans?

How large are the Revenues and Riches of their Princes? and in what do they Consist, and how Collected? . . .

How are their people generally employd? Whether they drive any Trade with their Neighbours, and if they do, what sort of Merchandise it is carryd on with?

What Commoditys their Country Yields, and the better to find this out 'twill be proper to Shew them Samples of Solid Gold, Gold Dust, Silver, Elephants Teeth, Gemms or any other valuable Commoditys; And if it appears by their Answers they have any of the first originaly in their Country, to be particular in finding out the manner of their Coming by it, whether They get it by washing the Earth after floods, as at Annamaboe, or by digging it out of Mines? . . .

The Middle Passage
But the white man's profits still turned on the precarious

Middle Passage. Captain Edward Hollden, master of a slaver, wrote this LETTER *despairingly to his employers.*

BARBADOS, Appril the 30th, 1723. *Sir,* This With My Humble Servis to you and the Rest of the Gentlemen Owners of the Ship *Grayhound* Galley and is to certifie you of my Arivall hear haveing seven Weeks Passage from Bony but very Dismall and Mortall for outt of 339 Slaves I brought in hear butt 214 for the Like Mortalaty I think Never was known for Jolly Likely Men Slaves to Eatt thair Diett over Night and the Nex Morning Dead 2 and 3 in a Night for severall Days after Wee Came from Bony as for Managementt I think

itt Could Nott be Better I allways had their Victtualls in good order and Took that Care to keep them and the Ship Sweet and Cleane allthoyt I Did itt my Self and Nott to Sufer any of them to Wett Their Foot on No Acctt: att my Arivall hear I aplyd my self to Mr. Crump and Heasell as Orderd I haveing on board aboutt 20 or 25 Slaves outt of flesh and do think itt for your Intrust to Leave them With Mr. Crump and Mr. Heasell for I think there Will be More Gain than Loss for to Run the Risk in Carrying them to Virginia and besids Discomodeing them as is in health. Provicions I have an Nought as Bread, beefe, Rice, beanes, yames so I Desire to Take in hear Sum Plantains a barrell of Flower a few Limes and sum Rum for a Recrute and so Make the best of My Way to Virginia as Directted . . . Gentellmen I Purchase att Bony 339 Slaves 189 Men and 128

17 *A slave coffle, escorted by black overseers, being marched from the African hinterland to the sea, to be sold to white dealers. Some coffles travelled as far as 600 miles*

Women 16 boys and 6 Girles I buried 17 before Came over the bar and 113 after Wards and have bought 28 Teeth Weighing between 15 and 16 hundred pound and Sum Red Wood. Dockter Smith is Dead and the Copper and four Sailors and one boy besides.

Instructions to Skippers

To the owners of slave ships, everything depended on engaging astute captains—men who would heed the manifold warnings heaped upon them. INSTRUCTIONS *from Isaac Hobhouse & Co, of Bristol, to Captain William Barry:*

BRISTOL, Oct. 7th, 1725. *Capt. Wm. Barry,* As the wind is inclineing to be fair you are ordered with yr. Men (which we allow to be 20 in Number yr self included) to repair on board the *Dispatch* Briggtn . . .

You must make the best of yr Way to the Coast of Africa that is to that part of it calld Andony [on the Bight of Biafra] (without toutching or tarrying at any other place) were you are to slave intirely . . .

The Cargo of goods are of your Own ordering, and as it's very good in kind and amts to thirteen hundred and thirty pounds eight shillings and $2\frac{1}{4}$ we hope twill purchase you 240 Choice slaves, besides a Quan'y of teeth the latter of which are always to embrace provided they are large, seeing in that Commodity there's no Mortality to be feard. As to the slaves let your endeavours be to buy none but what's healthy and strong and of a Convenient Age —none to exceed the years of 25 or under 10 if possible, among which so many men, and stout men boys as can be had seeing such are most Valuable at the Plantations.

Let your Care be in preserving so well as in purchaseing, in order to which let their provisions be well and Carefully look'd after and boild and that it's given them in due season, to see the sailors dont abuse them which has often been done to the prejudice of the Voyage. So soon as you begin to slave let your knetting be fix'd breast high fore and aft and so keep 'em shackled and hand Bolted fearing their rising or leaping Overboard, to prevent which let always a Constant and Carefull watch be appointed to which must give the strictest Charge for the preservation of their Own Lives, so well as yours and on which the Voyage depends, which per sleeping in their Watch has often been fatall and many a good Voyage (which otherwise might have been made) entirely ruind . . .

When you are fully slaved make the best of your way to Princess [a Portuguese-owned island north of São Tome] were you are to water and gett other Recruits that may want and there may dispose of all your returned goods for goold, as also so many or all of the slaves provided Can gett 10 moydores or upwards per head round, which if so make the best of your Way directly hither but in case you Cant then proceed to Antigua, were expect our farther orders in the hands of Capt. John Turnell which if should not find then repair to Newis at Mr. John Woodleys where if should also miss thereof, or either of the Islands, then make the best of your Way to So. Carolina and d'd all the slaves to Mr. Jos. Wragg who shall have directions for the farther proceedings.

Your Coast Comm'n is 4 from every £104 of the Net proceeds of the slaves etc, your privelidge slaves 2 provided you purchase 'em with your Own Goods and mark 'em in the presence of boathe Mates. [Officers were sometimes permitted free transport for one or several slaves which they sold on their own account.] Mr. Ross the Chief Mate has the same priviledge for his encouragemt but you must supply him with goods to doe it, which you are to take an Acct. of, as he must be debitted for it here at home after knows what 'tis, his slaves must also be marked in your presence and 2d Mate and as for

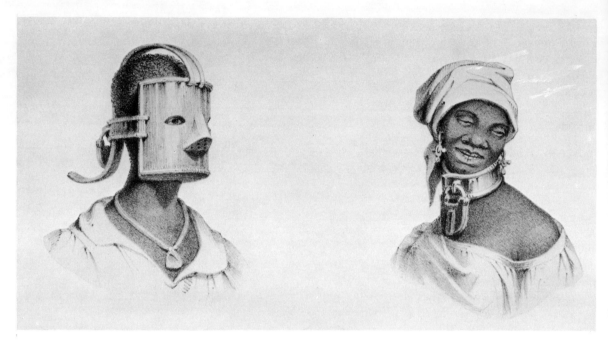

18 *Face muzzle and iron collar used by owners to punish slaves. Physical restraints were standard. Male slaves in transit from Africa were shackled to prevent insurrection or leaping overboard*

teeth We cant Allow to any. You must pay the half wages abroad accd'g to Act of Parliamt, and in all your Passages keep a good and Constant Look Out, and trust no sail you see fearing Pirates, see your Officers does their Duty in their severall stations and with them and the Men keep a good Harmony and decorum without to much familiarity or Austerity seeing the Voyage depends on good Conduct . . .

In case of Your Mortality (which God forbid) then its our directions Mr. Jno Ross take up and follow these our Instructions and after him Mr. Willm Pine 2d Mate.

Wee cant break of without recommending to you dispatch which is the Life of the Voyage and as you know that Commerce is ready and bound the same Way therefore endeavour w't in you lies to gett there before her and to see you are not outdone in the slaving by other Commanders.

be carefull of fire and in fine of all committed to your Charge, and keeping us advised by all Opportunitys of all materiall Occurrences is what imediatly offers but recommending you to the Good God Almighty's protection and wishing you a good Voyage we Remain

Yr Aff Fds

ISAAC HOBHOUSE
NO. RUDDOCK
WM. BAKER.

A Negro Petition

Slaves could sometimes buy their freedom by saving pittances earned from selling produce they grew on small plots allotted them by their masters. Others were actually given their freedom, sometimes because they

were no longer worth their keep, sometimes as rewards for meritorious service. Such emancipation was frequently written into wills. But the freed slave's status was always in question: it was generally assumed that if a man were black he was some white man's property. There are many records of freemen having to re-establish their manumission in the courts, as in the case of this North Carolina PETITION (1726):

To the Honoble Christopher Gale Esqr Chief Justice of the General Court February the third one thousand Seven hundred & twenty Six
The Complaint and petition of peter Vantrump a free Negro Sheweth that yor Complainant being a free Negro and at his own voluntary disposall & hath hired himself to Service Sundry times particularly in New York and other places and being at St Thomas's this Summer past one Captain Mackie in a Brigantine from thence being bound (as he reported) to Europe Your Honors Complainant agreed to go with him in Order to gett to Holland but instead of proceeding the Sayd Voyage the Sayd Mackie came to North Carolina where combining with one Edmund porter of this province and fearing the Sayd Mackie not to be on a lawfull Trade Yor Complainant was desirous to leave him and the Sayd porter by plausible pretences gott Your Complainant to come away from the Sayd Mackie with him although Your Complainant often told the Sayd porter that he was not a Slave but a free man Yet nevertheless the Sayd porter now against all right now pretends Your Complainant to be his Slave and hath held and used him as Such wherefore Your Complainant prays he may be adjudg^d & declar^d free as in Justice he ought to be & Sign^d Peter Vantrump.

Slavery in England
The slave's status provided a far more subtle problem in England, as planters began to retire from the West Indies, bringing their body servants home with them. Were they, on English soil, still legally slaves?

During the reign of the first Elizabeth, a certain Cartwright had 'brought a Slave from Russia, and would scourge him, for which he was questioned; and it was resolved, That England was too pure an Air for Slaves to breathe in'. In 1706 Lord Chief Justice Holt had concurred: '. . . As soon as a Negro comes into England he becomes free.'

Worried about their property, the repatriated planters, in 1729, applied to the law officers of the Crown for a reading. The Attorney General, Sir Philip Yorke, and the Solicitor General, Charles Talbot, produced a RULING which remained definitive for the next forty-three years.

We are of Opinion, that a Slave by coming from the West-Indies to Great Britain or Ireland either with or without his Master, doth not become free, and that his Master's Property or Right in him is not thereby determined or varied: And that Baptism doth not bestow freedom on him, nor make any Alteration in his Temporal Condition in these Kingdoms. We are also of Opinion, that his Master may legally compel him to return again to the Plantations.

P. YORKE
C. TALBOT
Jan. 14, 1729.

A Slave Mutiny
The negroes themselves fought for their freedom wherever and whenever they could. Slave risings at sea were commonplace. This account appeared in the Boston NEWS LETTER in 1731.

. . . I George Scott, (the Scriber) Master of the Sloop the *Little George*, belonging to Rhode Island; Saild from the Bonnana Islands on the Coast of Guinea, the first of June 1730, having on Board

Ninety six Slaves (thirty five of which were Men.) On the 6th of said Month at half an hour past four of the Clock in the Morning, being about 100 Leagues distant from the Land, the Men Slaves got off their Irons, and making way thro' the bulkhead of the Deck, killed the Watch consisting of John Harris Doctor, Jonathan Ebens Cooper, and Thomas Ham Sailor; who were, tis thought, all asleep. I being then in my Cabin and hearing a Noise upon Deck (they throwing the Watch overboard) took my Pistol directly, and fired up the Scuttle which was abaft, which made all the Slaves that were loose run forwards except one or two Men (who seemed to laugh at the Cowardice of the rest, and defiance of us, being but 4 Men and a Boy) who laid the Scuttle, and kept us down confin'd in the Cabin, and passing by the Companion to view us, we Shot two Men Slaves.

On so sudden a surprize, we were at a loss what to do, but consulting together, filled two round Bottles with Powder, putting Fuses to them, in order to send them among the Slaves, with a Design at the same instant of Time, to issue out upon them, and either suppress them or loose our Lives; but just as we were putting our design in Execution, one of the Slaves let fall an Ax (either thro' accident or design) which broke the Bottle as Thomas Dickenson was setting fire to the Fuze, and taking fire with a Cagg of Powder, in the Cabin, rais'd up the Deck, blew open the Cabin Doors and Windows, discharged all our fire Arms but one, distroyed our Cloathes and burnt the Man that had the Bottle in his hand in a most miserable manner, and my self with the rest very much hurt thereby.

Upon this unhappy accident, we expected no less than immediate Death, which would have been un-

avoidable, had they at that Juncture of time, rushed in upon us . . . we were resolved to withstand them to the uttermost; and accordingly Loaded our Arms and Shot several of the Slaves, which occasioned all the Men Slaves to betake themselves to the Quarter Deck, over our Heads. The Slaves then got two Swivel Guns, and filled them almost full with Powder . . . which they put fire to several times, but could not get off by reason of wet Weather. We had two Carriage Guns in the Boat, which we expected the Slaves would get out, and therefore watched them very narrowly; but in a dark Night they effected it, and brought them upon the Quarter Deck; they loaded one of the Guns, and pointed it directly down the Scuttle: we hearing them about the Scuttle and having prepar'd ourselves; so soon as they lifted it up, we Shot the Man dead that pointed the Gun, another of the Slaves standing by clapt a Match to it and fire'd it off, which blew the Scuttle all to pieces and some of the Deck, but did us no damage. They then took pieces of Boards and laid them over the Scuttle and the Hole they had made in the Deck, and laid the Tarpawlin, with a great Weight upon them, to prevent our coming up.

Then they made Sail . . . And the Fourth Day after the Rising made the same Land we departed from, then stood off and on again for 4 or 5 Days more, in which time the Boy being forced by Hunger, run up among the Slaves, who immediately put him in Irons. They made several attempts to come down into the Cabin, but their Courage fail'd them. I then call'd to them to come down to decide the Matter, they answer'd, by and by.

. . . we thought it proper before our Strength was quite spent to take some desperate Course. I proposed to cut away the Cieling and Bore some Holes thro' the Vessels Bottom . . . and let in about three feet of Water, I then called to the Slaves, and told them, I would drown them all . . . They then sent the

19 *Slave insurrections at sea were, after disease, the worst threat to crews. Most occurred within sight of the African coast. Here, blacks assault the* barricado, *from behind which seamen defend themselves with muskets*

Boy to the Cabin Door, to tell us, that they had but just made the Land, and that when they got a little nearer the Shore, they would take the Boat and leave them with the Young Slaves: I told them if they would do that I would not sink her . . . They stood in for the Land about 12 a Clock at Night, struck upon the Bar of Serrilone River, and were in great Danger of being lost. The Vessel being strong beat over the Bar, and they run Ashore about 3 Leagues up the River, on the North Side; being then High Water, and at Seven a Clock the next Morning there was not above a foot of Water along side.

The Natives waded from the Shore with fire Arms, wou'd have fain try'd to overcome us, but were perswaded from it by the Slaves on Board, who told them we should shoot them if they appeared in our Sight. They perswaded the grown Slaves to go Ashore, and drove the Young ones over board and then followed them, making the Vessel shake at their Departure . . . We found our great Guns loaded quite full. And as we hoisted out our Boat, the Natives mustered very thick on the Shore and fired at us divers time. We made what haste we could to the other side of the River, where we . . . found a Sloop riding in French-man's Bay belonging to Montserat, James Collingwood Commander, where we refreshed our selves . . . having had nothing to subsist upon, during the Nine Days we were under this Affliction but Raw Rice.

Slave Dealing in Africa

The lynch pins of slavery were the Europeans—the factors—stationed on the African coast, who, to serve the white traders, were forced to truckle to the slave-selling African kings. In many ways they were as much enslaved as the blacks who passed through their hands. Cooped up in the stench of their factories, neighbour to slaves within and contemptuous blacks without, their lives were 'solitary, poor, nasty, brutish and short'. They seldom survived more than two or three years. At this period, their annual pay was £30 a year, food and lodging supplied. Most were utterly degraded, but there were exceptions. A few left memorable EYE-WITNESS ACCOUNTS. *Among these was Francis Moore, an Englishman who worked for the Royal African Company, and dealt with nineteen riparian rulers along the Gambia River. His account refers to the period 1730–35:*

. . . The . . . [African] Merchants bring down Elephants Teeth, and in some Years Slaves to the Amount of 2000, most of which they say are Prisoners taken in War: They buy them from the different Princes who take them . . . Their Way of bringing them is, tying them by the Neck with Leather-Thongs, at about a Yard distance from each other, 30 or 40 in a String, having generally a Bundle of Corn, or an Elephant's Tooth upon each of their Heads . . .

Besides the Slaves which the Merchants bring down, there are many bought along the River. These are either taken in War, as the former are, or else Men condemn'd for Crimes, or else People stolen, which is very frequent. The Company's Servants never buy any of the last, if they suspect it, without sending for the Alcade, or chief Men of the Place, and consulting with them about the Matter. Since this Slave-Trade has been us'd, all Punishments are chang'd into Slavery; there being an Advantage on such Condemnations, they strain for Crimes very hard, in order to get the Benefit of selling the Criminal. Not only Murder, Theft and Adultery, are punish'd by selling the Criminal for a Slave, but every trifling Crime is punish'd in the same manner.

There was a Man brought to me in Tomany, to be sold for having stolen a Tobacco-pipe. I sent for the Alcade, and with much ado persuaded the Party grieved to accept of a Composition, and leave the Man free.

20 *Slaves being marched from the African interior to the coast often died from disease or attacks by wild beasts. Some committed suicide by eating earth*

In Cantore, a Man seeing a Tyger eating a Deer, which he had kill'd and hung up near his House, fir'd at the Tyger, and the Bullet kill'd a Man: The King not only condemn'd him, but also his Mother, three Brothers and three Sisters, to be sold. They were brought down to me at Yamyamacunda; it made my Heart ake to see them, and I did not buy them; upon which they were sent farther down the River, and sold to some separate Traders Ships at Joar, and the King had the Benefit of the Goods for which they were sold . . . The Slaves sold in the River, besides those brought by the Merchants, may amount in a Year to about 1000, more or less, according to the Wars upon the River . . .

CHAPTER THREE

Profiteers and Abolitionists (1736-76)

Yankee Slavers

North Americans were slow to enter the slave trade, although a few Dutch settlers had seized small numbers of negroes from Portuguese and Spanish vessels as early as the first third of the seventeenth century. Later, English colonists sailed as far as East Africa for blacks —considered less desirable than the West Coast tribes— to avoid conflict with the Royal African Company's monopoly.

It was not until 1723 that Yankees moved into the commerce on a large scale, with rum distilled from the molasses they took home in exchange for the wretched 'Jamaica quality' fish they sold as slave fodder in the Sugar Islands. Within a few years they were competing savagely, not only with the British and the French, but with each other, as this LETTER *from John Cahoone, a Rhode Island skipper, indicates.*

ANAMABO, Octobr the 27th, 1736.
Sir, After My Respects to you: these may Inform how it is with me at present. I bles god I Injoy my health very well as yett: but am like to have a long and trublesom Voyge of it, for there never was so much Rum on the Coast at one time before, Nor the like of the french shipen never seen before for no. for the hole Coast is full of them. for my part I can give no guess when I shall get away, for I purchest but 27 Slaves since I have bin hear, for Slaves is Very Scarce. we have had Nineteen sail of us at one time in the Rhoad: so that these ships that are said to Cary prime Slaves off is now forced to take any that Comes. heair is 7 sail of us Rume men that we are Ready to Devur one another; for our Case is Despart: So, I begg that you will exist my family in what they shall want for I no not when I shall git home: to them myself. I have had the misfortune to Bury my Chefe Mate on the 21st of September, and one man more; and lost the Negro man, primus, and Adam Over board on my pasedge one three weeks after another: that makes me now

Very weak handed: for out of what is left theair is two that is good for nothing. Cap Hamond hath bin heair six months and has but 60 Slaves on bord. my harty service to yr Spouse and family.

Attack on Slavery

Competition on the Coast reflected the prosperity which, for the Anglo-Americans, was to expand and endure through nearly seven decades. With growing wealth came growing criticism. In July 1740, THE GENTLE-MAN'S MAGAZINE *carried a contribution signed 'Mercator Honestus'.*

A Letter to the Gentlemen Merchants in the Guinea Trade, particularly addressed to the Merchants in Bristol and Liverpool.

21 *Bristol: the waterfront. Chronologically, Bristol's supremacy as a slaving port fell between those of London and of Liverpool*

GENTLEMEN,
I Am induced to consider the Nature of the *Guinea* Trade, as well with regard to the Welfare and Happiness of the *Britons*, as of the *Negroes*. For it is a Maxim with me, that whenever a Man acts wrong, I mean knowingly, he acts contrary to his true Interest; and if he acts wrong ignorantly, it would be better both for the Public and himself, that he were rightly informed.

I take it to be undoubtedly true, that all Mankind are brought into the World with a natural Right to Liberty, and that a Man cannot forfeit his Right to Liberty, but by attempting to take away the Property of another unjustly, in which I include his Life, Liberty and other Valuables; and that a Parent's meriting a Loss of Liberty, is no Reason why a Child, the Descendant from that Parent, shall lose its Liberty: But do not Persons in the *Guinea* Trade deal in Men, Women and Children? Moreover, in doing this it is evident they encourage the Negroes

to Acts of Hostility; nay, to take and enslave those with whom, perhaps, they had no Cause to be uneasy.

Children are made Slaves for Life who were not in a Capacity of losing their Liberty; and is it not in vain to urge the Sentiments of those from whom they buy them, or to assert that they would destroy, or eat them? For I don't doubt the Blacks are more civilized than they are generally represented, and it is very certain, that with some Pains they might become much more so. —— Besides, they are beyond Dispute, in general, in a more innocent State in their own Country than they are afterwards; for, as I take it, Countries they go to, have less of true Virtue and pure Religion than their own, and doubtless to die when less vicious is more a Mercy than to have Life, Existence here, prolonged in Vice and Wickedness. The hard Usage Negroes meet in the *West Indies* is also very shocking. A Pint of Corn and a Herring is all their Food for a long, hot, toilsome Day, where the unavoidable Loss of Spirits requires much more Refreshment than in *England*; and with Sorrow be it said, this Herring and Pint of Corn sometimes escape them . . .

The Chearfulness the Negroes shew in dying, proceeds not so much from Ignorance as from a Natural Nobleness of Soul, and the base Usage they meet with amongst those (tho' very improperly) called Christians. —— Some, I am not ignorant, object against all Trade, in order to vindicate the *Guinea* Trade; for, say they, if you deal in Linnen Checks, or Cotton Goods, or anything else sent abroad for the use of the Negroes, you are an Encourager of the *Guinea* Trade. But might not these Gentlemen with equal Reason object against having to do with Wine, or Ale, because some who are not in an honourable Way of Life, make use of these things?

I could heartily wish some Gentlemen would give the Public their Reasons why they carry on this

22 *John Locke, philosopher (1632-1704), one of the earliest anti-slavery spokesmen, called the institution a 'vile estate'*

Trade; for I doubt not there are wise and good Men concerned in it: Which Reasons, if good, will convince the wise and unprejudiced Part of the World. But if they have not good Reasons, I would beg of them to consider the Folly of acting unworthily for a little Gain . . .

A reply to 'Mercator Honestus' came the following December in THE LONDON MAGAZINE.

. . . there are People in some boasted Regions of Liberty, under a more wretched Slavery, than the Africans transplanted to our American Colonies.

The Inhabitants of Guinea are indeed in a most deplorable State of Slavery, under the arbitrary

23 *Daniel Defoe (1659?-1731). His Man Friday in* Robinson Crusoe *(1719) personified the 'noble savage'. He attacked slavery in* Reformation of Manners *(1702)*

Powers of their Princes both as to Life and Property. In the several Subordinations to them, every great Man is absolute lord of his immediate Dependents. And lower still; every Master of a Family is Proprietor of his Wives, Children, and Servants; and may at his Pleasure consign them to Death, or a better Market. No doubt such a State is contrary to Nature and Reason, since every human Creature hath an absolute Right to Liberty. But are not all arbitrary Governments, as well in Europe, as Africa, equally repugnant to that great Law of Nature? And yet it is not in our Power to cure the universal Evil, and set all the Kingdoms of the Earth free from the Domination of Tyrants . . .

. . . by purchasing, or rather ransoming the Negroes from their national Tyrants, and transplanting them under the benign Influences of the Law, and Gospel, they are advanced to much greater Degrees of Felicity, tho' not to absolute Liberty . . .

Perhaps my Antagonist calls the Negroes allowance of a Pint of Corn and an Herring, penurious, in Comparison of the full Meals of Gluttony: But if not let him compare that Allowance, to what the poor Labourer can purchase for Ten-pence per Day to subsist himself and Family, and he will easily determine the American's Advantage . . .

Nevertheless, Mercator will say, the Negroes are Slaves to their Proprietors: How Slaves? Nominally: Not really so much Slaves, as the Peasantry of all Nations is to Necessity; not so much as those of Corruption, or Party Zeal; not in any Sense, such abject Slaves, as every vicious Man is to his own Appetites . . .

Specifications for a Slave Ship

In the early years, slave quarters were improvised aboard existing ships. Later, vessels were purpose-built. A LETTER *from Joseph Manesty, a Liverpool slaving merchant, to John Bannister, an associate in Newport, Rhode Island, gives a detailed picture of slave-ship construction.*

LIVERPOOL Augt. 2d 1745.
Sir, I desire you will order Two Vessels built with the best white Oak timber at Rhode Island, both to-be Square stern'd with 2½ and 3 Inch plank with good substantial bends or Whales. they are for the Affrican Trade to have middling bottoms to have a full Harpin and to carry their Bodies well forward

and in the upper work not so much tumbled in as common for the more commodious stowing Negroes twixt Decks. To have snug heads without Rails, plain sterns, firm Quarter pieces no Quarter Windows nor Joiners work in the Cabbin (except so much as to sit in the Cabbin Windows) to Stern with a Tiller over the Round house to be sheath'd on the Stocks.

58 feet long in the Keel ⎫ Main Mast 60 feet long,
22 feet beam   ⎪ Main Yard 44 feet long,
10 feet hold   ⎬ Main Top Mast 30 feet
5 feet twixt Decks   ⎪ long all the other Masts and
                        ⎭ Yards in proportion, each
Yard Arm 2 feet a Rising on the Quarter Deck and fore Castle 10 inches, bulk heads to be a Solid beam a half Round house 12 feet long on the sheets, the Gun Wall on the Main Deck 14 Inches Solid, on the Quarter Deck and forecastle 4 Inches, but the Timbers left high enough to Support Rails all round the Vessel for Guns 2½ feet from the Gunell, the Round house to be 2½ feet higher than the Quarter Deck 5½ feet high in the inside under the Beams, to have the same rounding on the Top as the other Decks, for messing Negroes on lower deck laid fore and aft. let them be ready for launching in August next, to be Coated with Pitch and Tarr and I will send over Cordage, Sails, Anchors, Nails, and such a Cargoe as you shall order and will send a Master if required to go hence about April next.

2 Gun Ports Stern

Parliament Ends the Slave Monopoly
There was continuing and urgent pressure upon the government to throw the trade open to all. In an ACT *of 1750, Parliament ended the Royal African Company's monopoly.*

Whereas the Trade to and from Africa is very advantageous to Great Britain, and necessary for the supplying the Plantations and Colonies thereunto belonging with a sufficient Number of Negroes at reasonable Rates; and for that Purpose the said Trade ought to be free and open to all his Majesty's Subjects: Therefore be it enacted, and it is hereby enacted by the King's most Excellent Majesty, by and with the Advice and Consent of the Lords Spiritual and Temporal, and Commons, in this present Parliament assembled, and by the Authority of the same, That it shall and may be lawful for all his Majesty's Subjects to trade and traffick to and from any Port or Place in Africa, between the Port of Sallee in South Barbary, and the Cape of Good Hope, when, and at such Times, and in such Manner, and in or with such Quantity of Goods, Wares or Merchandizes, as he or they shall think fit . . .

John Newton's Log
Britons who chose to join the new Company of Merchants Trading to Africa paid a membership fee of forty shillings. In that same year, Britain sold the unexpired Asiento *back to the Spanish king for £100,000. By then Liverpool had outdistanced Bristol, which had earlier displaced London, and was now not only England's but the world's chief slaving port. In 1752, a total of eighty-eight Liverpool ships carried about 25,000 Africans to the Americas.*

Among the Liverpool skippers was John Newton, one of the strangest men in slavery's history. He sailed for the Guinea coast first as master of Duke of Argyll, *and later as master of a newly-built vessel,* African. *Self-confessed reprobate, drunkard and libertine, he grew to hate the trade as only a man who knew it could. He was to become not only co-author, with William Cowper, of the* Olney Hymns, *but rector of the church of St Mary Woolnoth, in the City of London, and a fiery abolitionist who strongly motivated William Wilberforce.* Duke of Argyll's LOG, *however, reveals only conventional aspects of slave-trading.*

REV.^D JOHN NEWTON,

late Rector of the United Parishes of St Mary Woolnoth & St Mary Woolchurch Haw.

Born at London 2.^d of July 1725. O.S. Died 21 of Decr 1807.

London Published as the Act directs 1 Jany 1808 by J.Smith 16 many Street Piccadilly.

24 *John Newton (1725-1807), slaver and self-styled libertine, who reformed, became rector of St Mary Woolnoth in London and preached against the trade*

Thursday 1st November [1750. Sierra Leone]. Fair hot weather, easy breases Easterly and calms. In the morning sent the punt on shoar with the carpenter, and the people [sailors] instead of returning on board went to the french Scooner and got drunk; after-

wards went on shoar to fight, which when they were sufficiently tired of, attempted to come off, but the ebb being made strong down, and they too drunk to pull well, came to a grapling amongst the rocks, so that when I sent Mr Marshall [second mate] to them in Captain Ellis's boat, he was obliged to slip the rope, not being able to purchase it. I was unluckily by their means deprived of a boat when I wanted to go on board to see Ord's slaves, by which means Ellis got 5, being all that were worth chusing. Gave two of my gentlemen a good caning and put one in irons, both for his behaviour in the boat and likewise being very troublesome last night, refusing to keep his watch and threatening the boatswain . . .

Saturday 3rd November. Fair weather, fresh land and sea brease. The carpenter finished his work on the longboat. In the morning had a visit from some Portuguese of Pirates bay, brought a woman slave, who I refused being long breasted, but dismissed them in very good humour with their reception, and they promise to bring me 2 young slaves in a little time . . .

Rhode Island Remonstrance to Westminster

Yankee traders had always maintained a stubborn separateness from their British counterparts. They bought and sold shrewdly, peddling slaves and slave fodder to the British Caribbean islands, but defiantly buying their sugar and molasses, the raw materials of their trade rum, primarily from the French, whose prices were lower. Aggrieved, the British planters lobbied Parliament which, in 1733, had laid heavy duties on all sugar and molasses imported to the North American mainland from anywhere but the British islands.

In response, the Yankees became smugglers; and the conflicts engendered led in large part to their eventual determination to cut free from the Mother Country. The first rumblings came from New England legislatures which petitioned Westminster for redress. In 1764, the

General Assembly of the colony of Rhode Island agreed upon a REMONSTRANCE *to the Board of Trade.*

. . . Formerly, the negroes upon the coast were supplied with large quantities of French brandies; but in the year 1723, some merchants in this colony first introduced the use of rum there, which, from small beginnings soon increased to the consumption of several thousand hogsheads yearly; by which the French are deprived of the sale of an equal quantity of brandy; and as the demand for rum is annually increasing upon the coast, there is the greatest reason to think, that in a few years, if this trade be not discouraged, the sale of French brandies there will be completely destroyed. This little colony, only, for more than thirty years past, have annually sent about eighteen sail of vessels to the coast, which have carried about eighteen hundred hogsheads of rum, together with a small quantity of provisions and some other articles, which have been sold for slaves, gold dust, elephants' teeth, camwood, etc. The slaves have been sold in the English islands, in Carolina and Virginia, for bills of exchange, and the other articles have been sent to Europe; and by this trade alone, remittances have been made from this colony to Great Britain, to the value of about £40,000, yearly. And this rum, carried to the coast, is so far from prejudicing the British trade thither, that it may be said rather to promote it; for as soon as our rum vessels arrive, they exchange away some of the rum with the traders from Britain, for a quantity of dry goods, with which each of them sort their cargoes to their mutual advantage.

Besides this method of remittance by the African trade, we often get bills of exchange from the Dutch colonies of Surinam, Barbice, etc., and this happens when the sales of our cargoes amount to more than

25 *A buyer on the African coast* (left) *examines a slave, while his comrade* (right) *exhibits trade goods to caboceers*

a sufficiency to load with molasses; so that, in this particular, a considerable benefit arises from the molasses trade, for these bills being paid in Holland, are the means of drawing from that republic so much cash yearly, into Great Britain, as these bills amount to.

From this deduction of the course of our trade, which is founded in exact truth, it appears that the whole trading stock of this colony, in its beginning, progress and end is uniformly directed to the payment of the debt contracted by the importation of British goods; and it also clearly appears, that without this trade, it would have been and always will be, utterly impossible for the inhabitants of this colony to subsist themselves, or to pay for any considerable quantity of British goods . . .

There are upwards of thirty distil houses, (erected at a vast expense; the principal materials of which, are imported from Great Britain,) constantly employed in making rum from molasses. This distillery is the main hinge upon which the trade of the colony turns, and many hundreds of persons depend immediately upon it for a subsistence. These distil houses, for want of molasses, must be shut up, to the ruin of many families, and of our trade in general; particularly, of that for the coast of Africa, where the French will supply the natives with brandy as they formerly did. Two-thirds of our vessels will become useless, and perish upon our hands; our mechanics, and those who depend upon the merchant for employment, must seek for subsistence elsewhere; and what must very sensibly affect the present and future naval power and commerce of Great Britain, a nursery of seamen, at this time consisting of twenty-two hundred, in this colony only, will be in a manner destroyed . . .

Tribal Wars and Slave Supply

Slavers on both sides of the Atlantic avidly watched African developments relevant to the fluctuating availability of blacks. The Newport, Rhode Island, MERCURY *reprinted an account from an English trader that first appeared in London, which described tribal wars obviously preluding a glut.*

July 10, 1765.
Our trade here has strangely altered within these six weeks. The long-talked of Shanty [Ashanti] expedition was at last effected in the following manner:

Sea Cooma, who succeeded Quishy, king of Ashanty, mustered an army (by the best intelligence we can get) of 60 [50] or 60,000 men, with which he marched against the Warsaws and Akims in April last, and drove them all down to the Fanty country: Here they have been skirmishing all the months of May and June, and on the 25th ult. after three or four days fighting, the Akims submitted to him, by which he immediately got possession of their camp, in which were all their women and children, and the greatest part of their men, to the number of about 15 or 20,000 in all . . .When the Akims and Shanties were fighting, the worthy Fanties were very busy, pillaging and stealing the Akims, who were so reduced by famine, that they gave themselves up in great numbers to any body that would promise them victuals, so that slaves became very plenty among these gentry, but they have not yet offered them for sale. Neither did they confine themselves to stealing the Akims only: For the Shanties began to pillage the Fanty crooms (towns) and plantations, by which conduct the Fanties picked up about 1000 of them, 300 of which we purchased in eight or nine days, in Castle Brew. Yan Woortman, who is chief of Cormantine purchased about 250 or 300 more; the remainder was bought by the ships at

26 *Granville Sharp (1735-1813), pioneer abolitionist. He established, through the courts, that slavery was illegal in England*

Cape Coast and Moore; we got ours at six ounces men, and four ounces women . . .

Abolition: The Somerset Case

So long as the buying, selling and owning of slaves proved economically sound, few—even those who were repelled by the brutality implicit—ventured to upset the trading pattern. Gradually, however, abolitionism gained impetus, not only through the basic humanitarianism of English society, but through its instinct to enshrine that humanitarianism within the law of the land.

England's first great abolitionist was Granville Sharp (1735–1813), a civil servant. His immediate and practical target was to invalidate the 1729 decision by the law officers of the Crown. In his view, their reading could not be legal in a country upon whose soil slavery had no positive legal existence. It took Sharp seven years and a string of law cases before he was able at last to convince the Lord Chief Justice, Lord Mansfield, to acknowledge the logic of his contention: that no man could hold property rights over another in England.

Lord Mansfield handed down his historic judgement on 22 June 1772, in the Court of King's Bench, in London. It was the first great step that was to lead to abolition throughout the world. The test trial involved the status of a slave, James Somerset, whose master, Charles Stewart, of Virginia, had brought him to England as his property. When Somerset tried to run away, Stewart had him kidnapped and put aboard a vessel in the Thames which would take him to Jamaica to be sold.

. . . The captain of the ship on board of which the negro was taken, makes his return to the writ [of Habeas Corpus on which the negro was released] in terms signifying that there have been, and still are, slaves to a great number in Africa; and that the trade in them is authorized by the laws and opinions of Virginia and Jamaica; that they are goods and chattels; and, as such, saleable and sold. That James Sommersett is a negro of Africa, and long before the return of the king's writ, was brought to be sold, and was sold to Charles Steuart, esq. then in Jamaica, and has not been manumitted since; that Mr. Steuart, having occasion to transact business, came over hither, with an intention to return; and brought Sommersett to attend and abide with him, and to carry him back as soon as the business should be transacted. That such intention has been, and still continues; and that the negro did remain till the time of his departure in the service of his master Mr. Steuart, and quitted it without his consent; and thereupon, before the return of the king's writ, the said Charles Steuart did commit the slave on board the Anne and Mary, to safe custody, to be kept till he should set sail, and then to be taken with him to Jamaica, and there sold as a slave. And this is the cause why he, captain Knowles, who was then and now is, commander of the above vessel, then and now lying in the river of Thames, did the said negro, committed to his custody, detain; and on which he now renders him to the orders of the Court. We pay all due attention to the opinion of sir Philip Yorke, and lord chancellor Talbot, whereby they pledged themselves to the British planters, for all the legal consequences of slaves coming over to this kingdom or being baptized, recognized by lord Hardwicke, sitting as chancellor on the 19th of October, 1749, that trover would lie: that a notion had prevailed, if a negro came over, or became a Christian, he was emancipated, but no ground in law: that he and lord Talbot, when attorney and solicitor-general, were of opinion, that no such claim for freedom was valid; that though the statute of tenures had abolished villeins regardant to a manor, yet he did not conceive but that a man might still become a

27 *William Murray, Lord Chief Justice Mansfield (1705-93), who ruled that slavery on English soil was unsupported by 'positive law'*

28 *Boston, Mass, early steam age. The port shared with Newport, RI, the bulk of American slave-trading, but southerners bought most of the blacks*

villein in gross, by confessing himself such in open court. We are so well agreed, that we think there is no occasion of having it argued (as I intimated an intention at first,) before all the judges, as is usual, for obvious reasons, on a return to a Habeas Corpus. The only question before us is, whether the cause on the return is sufficient? If it is, the negro must be remanded; if it is not, he must be discharged. Accordingly, the return states, that the slave departed and refused to serve; whereupon he was kept, to be sold abroad. So high an act of dominion must be recognized by the law of the country where it is used. The power of a master over a slave has been extremely different in different countries. The state of slavery is of such a nature, that it is incapable of being introduced on any reasons, moral or political, but only by positive law, which preserves its force long after the reasons, occasion, and time itself from whence it was created, is erased from memory. It is so odious, that nothing can be suffered to support it, but positive law. Whatever inconveniences, therefore, may follow from the decision, I cannot say this case is allowed or approved by the law of England; and therefore the black must be discharged.

Epitaph of a Slave

But Mansfield's writ ran only to the shore. Across the sea, nothing had changed. In 1773, only three years before the American Declaration of Independence, whose touch-stones were the freedom and equality of man, these bitter words were carved upon a tomb in Concord, Massachusetts:

GOD
Wills us free;
Man
Wills us slaves,

I will as God wills,
God's will be done.

Here lies the body of JOHN JACK,
A native of Africa, who died March, 1773,
Aged about *sixty years.*

Tho' *born* in a land of *slavery,*
He was born *free;*
Tho' he lived in a land of *liberty,*
He lived a *slave* . . .

Tho' not long before
Death, the grand Tyrant,
Gave him his final emancipation,
And set him on a footing with kings . . .

The American Rebels and the Trade

*Although England and the colonies were by now already
at war, many merchants still saw the conflict merely as
a threat to their livelihood rather than as a turning
point in history. Typical were the slavers, the narrow
limits of whose thinking are shown in passages from*
TWO LETTERS, *the first from John Fletcher, writing in
London to Captain Peleg Clarke of Newport, Rhode
Island, then at Anamabo; and the second from Clarke
to Fletcher.*

LONDON 29th Jany. 1776.
. . . in regard to America their Seems No likelyhood
of coming to Any Accomodation at presant, the
late act of Parliament pass'd will Stop up all their
Ports, And Men of Warr to take All their Shiping
will put a finishing Stroke to poor America, A great
Navy and Army going Over in the Spring, they must
submit I think at last, tho' I fear Not with out a
great loss, The Americans has fitted out several
Cruse'g Vessels and have taken Some of our Trans-
ports, and people here Are Affraid of the West
Indies Men coming home, wh has advanced the
premium of Insurance Double. I wish you had a
few Carriage Guns if it was but 4, for Self deffence,
perhaps you may get Some off the Ships on the
Coast to spare you that Number, every merchant-
man now carrys Guns the Same as in time of
War . . .

CAPE COAST ROADE 6 July 1776.
. . . I am excessive sorry to hear there is no likely-
hood of matters being Accomodated between Great
Britain and her Colonies, and likewise that such
Acts of Parliament pass'd, to take All the American
Vessels, for I assure you we had like to have been
taken off the Coast, from the orders the Men of
Warr had dated Octr. 11th 1775; had I not keeped
out of the way All the time the Menawar were on
the Coast. And I have been in the greatest Dilemma
Imaginable About the Acts, and what to do with the
Vessel, As I never durst take Any Slaves on board
not thinking the Intrest safe to be brought off in her,
Untill a few days ago I found Some Exemtions from
Acts pass'd to take All Americans, in the publick
Ledger of Feb'y 7th (*viz.* Exemption 4th) is Ships
cleared out from any port of Great Britain or Ireland
before the 1st Jany. 1776 for Any of the British Sugar
Colonies in the West Indies, and Ships cleared out
from the Said British Colonies and bound to Great
Britain or Ireland, Provided 2/3 of the owners of
Such Ships as [are] His Majestys Subjects Residing
in Great Britain or Ireland, or Some of the Said
Sugar Colonies. The Above Act entirely Acquits us,
as we are cleared out for Jamaica, and Coppy of Our
Register Sent to Montego Bay, will entirely Acquit
us from farther trouble.

Your paragraph Concerning geting a few Guns
on Account of the American privateers, there is none
to be gott, Every body that has any do not chuse to
part with them for the Same Reasons, And for my
part I do not think but that the American Privateers
are So large that 4 or 6 Guns would be of little use,
if to be had. You better know what danger there is
of privateers than I do, So beg you will Insure my
Intrest [f]or as much as you think prudent, but as
our Stay on the Coast will be so long, I am in great
hopes Every thing may be Setled before we Reach
the W. Indies, and That Great Britain and her
Colonies may be Unitted in a Everlasting Union, Is
my Sincere Wish . . .

29 Drafters of Declaration of Independence which
guaranteed 'life, liberty and the pursuit of happiness' –
except to slaves. Standing, Benjamin Franklin (1706-90).
Others (l to r), Thomas Jefferson (1743-1826), Robert R.
Livingston (1746-1813), John Adams (1735-1826) and
Roger Sherman (1721-93)

CHAPTER FOUR

The Trade in Retreat (1781-1807)

The "Zong" Case

The War of Independence (1775–83) spelled hard times for the trade. British and American privateers preyed upon each other's ships, and American ports were closed to all British commerce. British slavers, therefore, could not dispose of as many slaves as they could buy in Africa. To this glut is owed the single most horrifying occurrence in the trade's history.

When the skipper of a Liverpool vessel, William *(owned by a leading firm, Messrs Gregson, Case, Wilson and Aspinall), found supplies at Anamabo over-plentiful, he bought on the spot a second ship,* Zong, *to carry a second black cargo to the West Indies. He appointed as master* William's *surgeon, Luke Collingwood. During the voyage, many of the slaves became ill and Collingwood hit upon the idea of throwing 150 of them overboard, so that insurance could later be claimed for their value. The reason he gave was that drinking water was short, and that the sickliest slaves had to be sacrificed to save the rest.*

When the claim was made—£30 per slave—the insurers refused to pay, and the dispute came before Lord Mansfield. Although Collingwood himself was by then dead, his plan did not miscarry: Zong's *owners won. Granville Sharp sent a* SUMMATION *of the case both to the Admiralty and to the Prime Minister, the Duke of Portland, on 18 July 1783:*

The ship *Zong*, or *Zung*, Luke Collingwood master, sailed from the island of St. Thomas, on the coast of Africa, the 6th September, 1781, with four hundred and forty slaves (or four hundred and forty-two) and seventeen Whites on board, for Jamaica; and on the 27th November following she fell in with that island; but, instead of proceeding to some port, the master, either through ignorance or a sinister intention, ran the ship to leeward, alleging that he mistook Jamaica for Hispaniola.

Sickness and mortality had by this time taken place, which is almost constantly the case on board slave-ships, through the avarice of those most detestable traders, which induces them to crowd, or rather to pack, too many slaves together in the holds of their ships; so that on board the *Zong*, between the time of her leaving the coast of Africa and the 29th of November 1781, sixty slaves and upwards, and seven White people, died; and a great number of remaining slaves, on the day last mentioned, were sick of some disorder or disorders, and likely to die, or not to live long.

. . . the dead and dying slaves would have been a dead loss to the owners, and, in some proportion, a loss also to the persons employed by the owners, unless some pretence or expedient had been found to throw the loss upon the insurers, as in the case of Jetsam or Jetson—*i.e.* a plea of necessity to cast

overboard some part of a cargo to save the rest. These circumstances, I say, are necessary to be remarked, because they point out the most probable inducement to this enormous wickedness.

The sickness and mortality on board the *Zong*, previous to the 29th November 1781 (the time when they began to throw the poor Negroes overboard alive), was not occasioned by the want of water; for it was proved that they did not discover till that very day, the 29th November (or the preceeding day) that the stock of fresh water was reduced to two hundred gallons: yet the same day, or in the evening of it, "before any soul had been put to short allowance", and before there was any present or real want of water, "the master of the ship called together a few of the officers, and told them to the following effect:—that, if the slaves died a natural death, it would be the loss of the owners of the ship; but if they were thrown alive into the sea, it would be the loss of the underwriters": and, to palliate the in-

30, 31 *Josiah Wedgwood (1730-95), English potter and ardent abolitionist, who sent a shipment of his firm's anti-slavery cameos* (right) *to Benjamin Franklin for distribution in the United States*

human proposal, he the said Collingwood pretended, that "it would not be so cruel to throw the poor sick wretches (meaning such slaves) into the sea, as to suffer them to linger out a few days under the disorders with which they were afflicted, or expressed himself to the like effect." To which proposal the mate (whose name is Colonel James Kelsal) objected, it seems, at the first, and said "there was no present want of water to justify such a measure": But "the said Luke Collingwood prevailed upon the crew, or the rest of them, to listen to his said proposal; and the same evening, and two or three or some few following days, the said Luke Collingwood picked, or caused to be picked out, from the cargo of the same ship, one hundred and thirty-three slaves [the figure claimed in court was 150], all or most of whom were sick or weak, and not likely to live; and ordered the crew by turns to throw them into the sea; which most inhuman order was cruelly complied with." I am informed, by a memorandum from the deposition of Kelsal the chief mate (one of the murderers), that fifty-four persons were actually thrown overboard alive on the 29th of November; and that forty-two more were also thrown overboard on the 1st December. And on this very day, 1st December, 1781, before the stock of water was consumed, there fell a plentiful rain, which, by the confession of one of their own advocates, "continued a day or two, and enabled them to collect six casks of water, which was full allowance for eleven days, or for twenty-three days at half-allowance"; whereas the ship actually arrived at Jamaica in twenty-one days afterwards—*viz.* on the 22d December, 1781. They seem also to have had an opportunity of sending their boat for water no less than thirteen days sooner, *viz.* on the 9th December, when they "made the west end of Jamaica, distant two or three leagues only," as I am informed by a person who was on board: and yet, notwithstanding this proof of a possibility that they might perhaps obtain further

supplies by rain, or that they might be able to hold out with their new-increased stock of water till they might chance to meet with some ship, or be able to send to some island for a further supply, they nevertheless cast twenty-six more human persons alive into the sea, even after the rain, whose hands were also fettered or bound; and which was done, it seems, in the sight of many other unhappy sufferers that were brought up upon deck for the same detestable purpose, whereby ten of these miserable human creatures were driven to the lamentable necessity of jumping overboard, to avoid the fettering or binding of their hands, and were likewise drowned . . .

George Washington on Slave-Owning
Across the Atlantic, the same question of whether a slave was a human being or merely property was exercising the new nation. George Washington, a slave-owner himself, commented on the dilemma in a LETTER *(dated 1786) to Robert Morris, a signatory of the Declaration of Independence.*

Dear Sir: I give you the trouble of this letter at the instance of Mr. Dalby of Alexandria; who is called to Philadelphia to attend what he conceives to be a vexatious lawsuit respecting a slave of his, whom a Society of Quakers in the city (formed for such purposes) have attempted to liberate . . . if the practice of this Society of which Mr. Dalby speaks, is not discountenanced, none of those whose *misfortune* it is to have slaves as attendants, will visit the City if they can possibly avoid it; because by so doing they hazard their property; or they must be at the expence (and this will not always succeed) of providing servants of another description for the trip.

I hope it will not be conceived from these observations, that it is my wish to hold the unhappy people, who are the subject of this letter, in slavery. I can only say that there is not a man living who wishes

32 *George Washington (1732-99), first president of the United States. He opposed slavery, but owned slaves*

more sincerely than I do, to see a plan adopted for the abolition of it; but there is only one proper and effectual mode by which it can be accomplished and that is by Legislative authority; and this, as far as my suffrage will go, shall never be wanting. But when slaves who are happy and contented with their present masters, are tampered with and seduced to leave; when a conduct of this sort begets discontent on one side and resentment on the other, and when it happens to fall on a man, whose purse will not measure with that of the Society, and he looses his property for want of means to defend it; it is oppression in the latter case, and not humanity in any, because it introduces more evil than it can cure.

Liverpool's Petition for Trade Protection
Anti-slavery sentiment was growing. In the United

States, Rhode Island's lower house passed history's first bill prohibiting the trade; this was, however, mutilated into impotence by the upper house. In England, abolitionists banded together in a society. Among their leaders were a number of clergymen, including John Newton, now thundering against the institution from the pulpit of St Mary Woolnoth; William Wilberforce; Thomas Clarkson, the movement's chief investigator; a group of Quakers, and Granville Sharp, the organisation's first chairman. With William Pitt the Younger, himself an abolitionist, in Downing Street, and his close friend Wilberforce pushing hard in Parliament, the government began to assume an anti-slavery posture. To counter the possibility of legislation which might inhibit the trade, the mayor and council of Liverpool, then starting the bumper years of her slaving career (878 Merseyside ships carried 303,737 negroes to the New World, worth £11,186,850, between 1783 and 1793), petitioned Westminster in 1788.

. . . That the trade of Liverpool having met with the countenance of this [your?] honourable House in many Acts of Parliament, which have been granted at different times during the present century, for the constructing of proper and convenient wet docks for shipping, and more especially for the African ships, which from their form require to be constantly afloat, your Petitioners have been emboldened to lay out considerable sums of money and to pledge their Corporate Seal for other sums to a very large amount for effectuating these goods [good?] and laudable purposes.

That your Petitioners have also been happy to see the great increase and different resources of trade which has flowed in upon their town by the numerous canals and other communications from the interior parts of this kingdom . . .

And that from these causes, particularly the convenience of the docks, and some other local advantages, added to the enterprizing spirit of the

33 *Thomas Clarkson (1760-1846) conducted a one-man abolitionist investigation. Abuses he uncovered affected parliamentary legislation*

34 *Liverpool. Negroes for domestic use were auctioned from the steps of the Custom House* (left). *By 1800, the port handled ninety per cent of the world's slave trade*

people, which has enabled them to carry on the African Slave Trade with vigour, the town of Liverpool has arrived at a pitch of mercantile consequence which cannot but affect and improve the wealth and prosperity of the kingdom at large.

Your Petitioners therefore contemplate with real concern the attempts now making . . . to obtain a total abolition of the African Slave trade . . . Your Petitioners humbly pray to be heard by their Counsel against the abolition of this source of wealth before the Honourable House shall proceed to determine upon a point which so essentially concerns the welfare of the town and port of Liverpool in par-

ticular, and the landed interest of the kingdom in general, and which in their judgment must also tend to the prejudice of the British manufacturers, must ruin the property of the English merchants in the West Indies, diminish the public revenue and impair the maritime strength of Great Britain . . .

The Dolben Act

Prime Minister William Pitt, however, committed the Commons to consider the slavery question in its next session. In anticipation, he ordered an inquiry into the trade by the Privy Council. Wilberforce was then preparing the first of his many attempts to force Parliament to forbid the trade; but he was delayed by illness from presenting his resolution. Meanwhile, Sir William Dolben, the member for Oxford, having seen on a slave

35 *Sir William Dolben (1727-1814), whose parliamentary bill, the Dolben Act, improved slave accommodations during the Middle Passage*

ship in the Thames how inhumanly the Africans were packed aboard, brought in an ameliorating Bill which was passed on 30 June 1788. It was the first PARLIAMENTARY ACT *to touch upon the workings of the trade.*

An Act to regulate, for a limited time, the shipping and carrying of slaves in British vessels from the coast of Africa.

Whereas it is expedient to regulate the shipping and carrying of slaves in British vessels from the coast of Africa; be it therefore enacted; and it is hereby enacted by the King's most excellent majesty, by and with the advice and consent of the lords spiritual and temporal, and commons, in this present parliament assembled, and by the authority of the same, That it shall not be lawful for any master, or other person taking or having the charge or command of any British ship or vessel whatever, which shall clear out from any port of this kingdom from and after the first day of August one thousand seven hundred and eighty eight, to have on board, at any one time, or to convey, carry, bring, or transport slaves from the coast of Africa to any parts beyond the sea, in any such ship or vessel, in any greater number than in the proportion of five such slaves for every three tons of the burthen of such ship or vessel, over and above the said burthen of such ship or vessel, so far as the said ship or vessel shall not exceed two hundred and one tons; and moreover, of one such slave for every additional ton of such ship or vessel, over and above the said burthen of two hundred and one tons, or male slaves who shall exceed four feet four inches in height, in any greater number than in the proportion of one such male slave to every one ton of the burthen of such ship or vessel, so far as the said ship or vessel shall not exceed two hundred and one tons, and (moreover) of three such male slaves (who shall exceed the said height of four feet four inches) for every additional five tons of such ship or vessel, over and above the said burthen of two hundred and one tons . . .

II. Provided always, That if there shall be, in any such ship or vessel, any more than two fifth parts of the slaves who shall be children, and who shall not exceed four feet four inches in height, then every five such children (over and above the aforesaid proportion of two fifths) shall be deemed and taken to be equal to four of the said slaves within the true intent and meaning of this act . . .

The Act went on to specify that masters and surgeons must keep accurate records of the number of slaves

PLAN AND SECTIONS OF A SLAVE SHIP.

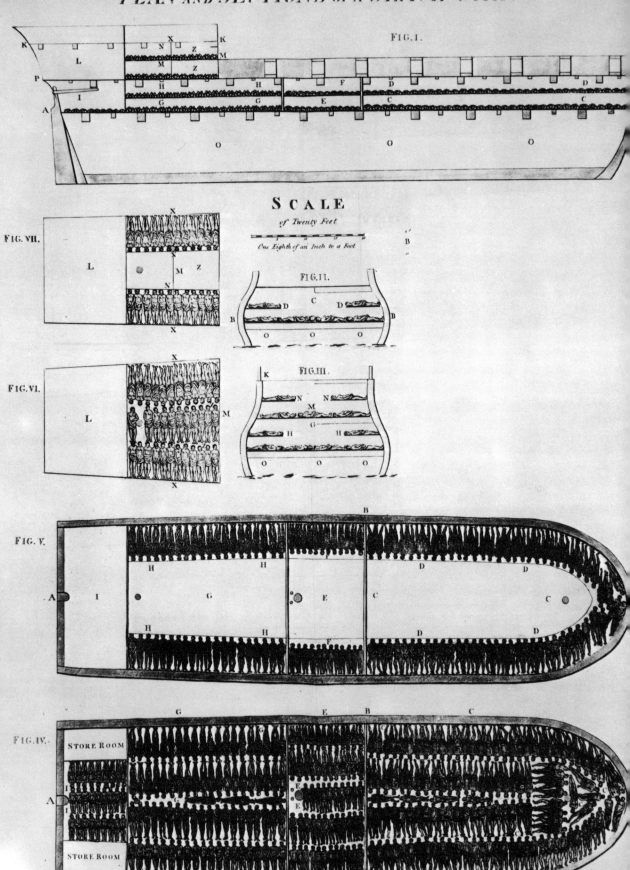

FIG. I.

SCALE
of Twenty Feet

One Eighth of an Inch to a Foot

FIG. VII.

FIG. VI.

FIG. II.

FIG. III.

FIG. V.

FIG. IV.

STORE ROOM

STORE ROOM

loaded, and of the number who died; that no cargo other than slaves be stowed on slave decks, and that (forestalling any repetition of the Zong tragedy) slaves could not be insured except against perils of the sea, piracy, insurrection, capture, barratry and fire. It also provided rewards for masters and surgeons who completed passages during which no more than three per cent of their slaves were lost.

The Select Committee on the Slave Trade

The Privy Council's examination of the trade was completed in 1789, but Parliament decided to re-conduct and expand the investigation. Witnesses both pro and con were questioned during 1789 and 1790, partly under Wilberforce's guidance. The result, a massive eye-witness document, MINUTES OF THE EVIDENCE DELIVERED BEFORE A SELECT COMMITTEE OF THE WHOLE HOUSE TO WHOM IT WAS REFERRED TO CONSIDER OF THE SLAVE TRADE, *was presented in 1791. It constitutes the single most important body of research available to the student. The following interrogations demonstrate the type of information furnished to the legislators:*

Lunae, 8° die Martii, 1790.

MR. ALEXANDER FALCONBRIDGE was called in, and examined.

What is your present situation?
A surgeon.

How many voyages have you been to the Coast of Africa...?
I have been four voyages to the Coast of Africa...

Do you examine the slaves previous to purchasing them?

36 *Plan for stowing slaves aboard* Brookes *of Liverpool: length 100ft, beam 25ft 4in, tonnage 320. Like most slavers, she had a platform between decks for capacity loading. On one voyage, extra platforms doubled the load shown here to 609. Slaves beneath and on the platforms could not sit upright*

They are always examined by some officers on board; it is generally understood to be the surgeon's business.

Do they appear dejected when brought on board?
All that I have seen in my voyages did appear so.

Did this dejection continue, or did it soon wear off?
With some it continued the whole voyage, and with others till death put a period to their misery.

Have you known instances of Slaves refusing sustenance?
I have known several instances.

With what design...?
With a design to starve themselves, I am persuaded.

Are compulsive means used to induce the Slaves to take their food?
In every ship that I have been, it has been the case.

Have you ever known them refuse to take their medicines when sick?
I have known many instances of it.

With what intention do you imagine?
With the same intention that they refused their food—that they would wish to die. I had a woman on board the Alexander, who was dejected from the moment she came on board; she was taken ill of a dysentery, and would neither take food or medicines: I often tried to make her swallow wine, but never could. I desired the interpreter to ask her what she wanted, or what I should get for her; she replied, she wanted nothing but to die—and she did die...

What was the mode used in stowing the Slaves in their night apartments?...
They had not so much room as a man has in his

coffin, neither in length or breadth, and it was impossible for them to turn or shift with any degree of ease. I have had occasion very often to go from one side of their rooms to the other; before I attempted it I have always taken off my shoes, and notwithstanding I have trod with as much care as I possibly could to prevent pinching them, it has unavoidably happened that I did so; I have often had my feet bit and scratched by them, the marks of which I have now . . .

Have you ever observed that the confinement in this situation has been injurious to the health of the Slaves?

So much so, that I have known them go down apparently in good health at night, and found dead in the morning. In my last voyage I remember a very stout man going down in the evening, to all appearance in good health, and he was found dead in the morning; I had the curiosity to open him, Mr. Fraser [the master] permitting that, provided it was done with decency: after all the Slaves were off the deck I opened the thorax and abdomen, and found the respective contents in a healthy state; I therefore conclude he must have been suffocated, or died for want of fresh air.

Were you ever yourself below when the Slaves were there; and describe the effects you perceived from it.

It is the surgeon's business to go below every morning the first thing; and I was never amongst them above ten minutes, but my shirt was as wet as if it had been dipt in water. In the Alexander, in coming out of the River Bonny, the ship got on ground on the Bar, she hung on her rudder, and detained us there six or seven days in consequence;

during that time there was a great swell, and a good deal of heavy rain; the air-ports were obliged to be shut, and part of the gratings on the weather side of her covered; almost all the men Slaves were taken ill with the flux [dysentery], I went down repeatedly amongst them; the last time that I went down it was so extremely hot that I took off my shirt, upwards of twenty of them had fainted, or were fainting. I got several of them hauled upon deck, and two or three of them died, and most of the rest before I arrived in the West Indies. I think I had been down about fifteen minutes, and it made me so very ill, that I could not get up without assistance. I was taken ill of a dysentery myself, and was unable to do my duty the whole passage afterwards . . .

Have you known the Slaves to suffer from the want of better accommodation?

They suffer exceedingly, especially those who are much emaciated, so much so, that I have seen the prominent part of their bones about the shoulder-blade and knees frequently bare—if I have put any kind of plaister or bandage on them, they generally remove them, and apply them to other purposes.

What are the most prevalent disorders on board a Negro ship?
I believe fevers and dysenteries.

Are the consequences ever extremly noxious and nauseous of great numbers being ill at once of this latter disorder?

It was the case in the Alexander, as I have said before when I was taken ill—I cannot conceive any situation so dreadful and disgusting, the deck was covered with blood and mucus, and approached nearer to the resemblance of a slaughter-house than anything I can compare it to, the stench and foul air were likewise intolerable . . .

Do those who are sick under these circumstances often recover?

37 *William Blake (1757-1827) reviled slavery both in pictures (left) and in poems such as 'The Little Black Boy' which conveyed an African child's feelings on seeing a white child*

I never myself could recover one who had a bad dysentery, nor do I believe the whole college of physicians, if they were there, could be of the least service, for I humbly conceive a disease cannot be cured while the cause remains.

What do you apprehend to be the main cause?

I think the principal causes are a diseased mind, sudden transitions from heat to cold, breathing a putrid atmosphere, wallowing in their own excrement, and being shackled together.

On what grounds do you ascribe the sickness of the [male] Slaves in any degree to the circumstances of their being shackled?

From their dying in above twice the number of the women, who are not shackled . . .

Have you known any other inconveniences resulting from their being thus shackled?

The inconvenience is great. In each apartment are placed three or four tubs, more or less; the Slaves that are at the greatest distance from these tubs find it very difficult to get over the other Slaves to them; and sometimes when one wants to go his companion will not agree to go with him; and while they are disputing, if one of them happens to be a little relaxed, he exonerates over his neighbours, which is the cause of great disturbance.

Have you ever known an instance of a Slave dying whilst still shackled to another?

In the Alexander I have known two or three instances of a dead and living Slave being found in the morning shackled together . . .

Have you known any instances of Slaves destroying themselves?

In my last voyage at Bonny, we had a fine young woman brought on board, who was continually crying, and was emaciated very much in the course of three or four days; she refused her food: it was thought proper, for the recovery of her health, to send her on shore to the town of Bonny; I was informed that she soon got chearful again; but hearing by accident she was to be sent on board the ship, she hung herself . . .

Did you ever know instances of insanity among the Slaves on board ship?

In my first voyage to Bonny, in the Alexander, I went on board the Amelia, then lying in the river, and which was about to sail; I saw a woman chained on deck, and I asked the chief mate what was the matter with her; he said she was mad.

Do you recollect any other instance?

I recollect, on my second voyage in the Amelia, we had a woman on board, whom we were forced to chain at certain times; at other times she appeared perfectly well; and, in one of those intervals, she was sold at Port Maria, in Jamaica.

To what cause do you describe the insanity in these instances?

To their being torn from their nearest connections, and carried away from their country.

How are the male Slaves secured when on deck?

While lying on the coast, as they come up in the morning a person examines their irons, and a large chain is reeved through a ring on the shackles of each, and through the ring-bolts on deck, and locked.

Do the male Slaves ever dance under these circumstances?

After every meal they are made to jump in their irons but I cannot call it dancing . . .

Is compulsion ever used, to make the Slaves take the exercise of dancing?

I have often been desired myself, in all the ships which I have been in, to flog such as would not jump or dance voluntarily . . .

38 *The 'cat-o'nine-tails', source of terror to seamen, was also used to punish slaves. Here, a wife is flogged for objecting to being sold separately from her husband. (Rear), slaves being marched off by new owners, and recalcitrant captive hanging from tree*

Have you ever known the Slaves sing when on board the ship?

I have.

Did you ever hear what was the subject of their songs?

I have desired the interpreter at Bonny to ask what they were singing about; and he has always told me, they were lamenting the loss of their country and friends . . .

Lunae, 10° die Maii 1790.

ISAAC PARKER, ship-keeper on board the Melampus frigate in ordinary, called in; and examined.

Were you ever in Africa?
Yes.

How often, when, and in what ship?
Three times; once in the Black Joke, in the year 1764, captain Joseph Pollard, from Liverpool, to the river Gambia: we slaved at Culloreen.

How were the Slaves treated in that voyage?
The Slaves were treated very well, except one child that was used ill.

39, 40, 41   *In the Sugar Islands, slaves are landed* (above left)*, examined and sold* (below left) *and finally put to work in the fields* (above) *under the whip of the driver or overseer*

Did captain Pollard command the ship during the whole of your voyage?

No; he died off the island of St. Jago, and captain Marshall, who was the chief mate, succeeded to the command . . .

Was the child to which you refer ill-treated by captain Pollard or captain Marshall?

By captain Marshall.

What were the circumstances of this child's ill treatment?

The child took sulk, and would not eat.

What followed?

The captain took the child up in his hand, and flogged it with the cat.

Did he say anything when he did so?

Yes; he said, "Damn you, I will make you eat, or I will kill you."

Could the Slaves who were on board see the captain while he was flogging the child?

Yes; they could.

How could they see him, and how did they behave on the occasion?

They saw it through the barricado, looking through the crevices; they made a great murmuring, and did not seem to like it.

Do you remember anything more about this child?

Yes; the child had swelled feet; the captain desired the cook to put on some water to heat to see if he could abate the swelling, and it was done. He then ordered the child's feet to be put into the water, and the cook putting his finger into the water, said, "Sir, it is too hot." The captain said, "Damn it, never mind it, put the feet in," and so doing the skin and nails came off, and he got some sweet oil and cloths and wrapped round the feet in order to take the fire out of them; and I myself bathed the feet with oil, and wrapped the cloths around; and laying the child on the quarter deck in the afternoon at mess time, I gave the child some victuals, but it would not eat; the captain took the child up again, and flogged it, and said, "Damn you, I will make you eat," and so he continued in that way for four or five days at mess time, when the child would not eat, and flogged it, and he tied a log of mango, eighteen or twenty inches long, and about twelve or thirteen pound weight, to the child by a string round its neck. The last time he took the child up and flogged it, and let it drop out of his hands, "Damn you (says he) I will make you eat, or I will be the death of you;" and in three quarters of an hour after that the child died. He would not suffer any of the people that were on the quarter deck to heave the child overboard, but he called the mother of the child to heave it overboard. She was not willing to do so, and I think he flogged her; but I am sure that he beat her in some way for refusing to throw the child overboard; at last he made her take the child up, and she took it in her hand, and went to the ship's side, holding her head on one side, because she would not see the child go out of her hand, and she dropped the child overboard. She seemed to be very sorry, and cried for several hours . . .

Slave Revolt on Santo Domingo

Having confronted the House with the MINUTES OF THE EVIDENCE, *Wilberforce, on 18 April 1791, moved to forbid further importation of slaves into the West Indies. But the pro-slavery forces remained powerful, and the Bill was defeated by 183 to 88. This mood intensified when news reached London that negroes on the French island of Santo Domingo (Hispaniola) had risen in revolt.*

The dynamics of their rebellion lay in the dynamics of the French revolution. Jacobin radicals had spoken out in favour of abolition. Although in practice they had done nothing, the scent of freedom proved heady on the island. Pro-slavers could now argue that even to talk of freedom was dangerous.

This article appeared in THE TIMES *of 28 October 1791.*

INSURRECTION AT SAINT DOMINGO

The dreadful slaughter committed between the inhabitants of this unfortunate island is confirmed in every respect by the letters received yesterday from France, nor does the havoc said to be committed among the negroes appear to be contradicted by good authority. The damage done to the plantations is infinitely greater that [sic] what was reported in our paper of yesterday.

The following is the whole substance of the letter written by Commodore AFFLECK at Jamaica to Mr. Stephens at the Admiralty, brought over by the Daphne frigate, Capt. Gardner.

The letter states, that, upon the information of a serious insurrection having broken out among the negroes and people of colour at ST. DOMINGO, Admiral AFFLECK went down with two frigates, the *Blonde* and the *Alert*, with the hopes of affording some assistance to the inhabitants; but finding this impractical in an effectual manner, he returned to Jamaica, and dispatched the *Daphne* to England with the information . . .

The letter farther relates, that the insurgents were encamped near the capital to the number of 35,000 people, 4000 of whom were armed with muskets, supplied by the Dutch and Spaniards; the remainder were armed with pitchforks and other weapons. The inhabitants had all retired within the fort, where they might remain in safety until some relief arrived.

42 *West Indian slaves, whenever they could, escaped into the hills and set up guerrilla communities. Called 'maroons', these rebels instigated many island insurrections*

The troops declined taking any part, and the Spaniards chose to give the appearance of preserving a perfect neutrality, although they are strongly suspected of having fomented the disturbances. It is hoped the want of provisions and stores for so large a body would oblige the insurgents to return to their duty. The ravages they had committed are very great; about 300 white people had been murdered, and upwards of two hundred sugar and coffee plantations were destroyed.

43 *Sugar Island planters, fearful for their own lives, hanged slaves for such serious crimes as insurrection. They displayed their severed heads as a warning to others*

Thus much appears by Commodore AFFLECK'S letter to MR. STEPHENS. By other channels of information we learn, that the white people at St. Domingo had dispatched a ship to America praying for assistance. That on the news of the insurrection being received at *Jamaica*, LORD EFFINGHAM has collected all the troops together, to be ready on the first alarm, and it was expected that MARTIAL LAW would be proclaimed ...

The event that has happened at ST. DOMINGO was apprehended by all well informed Frenchmen. The decree of the last French legislature, *placing the people*

of colour on an equality with the whites—had been the principal cause of the mischief that ensued. M. de BARNAVE used his influence before the last Assembly dissolved itself, to get that decree repealed. He repeatedly warned the Diet of the consequences that would result, and his ideas are now verified . . .

If the rebellion should grow more serious at ST. DOMINGO, it is most certain that the inhabitants will invite some foreign power to come and take possession of them . . . From the calamities one has suffered from French intrigues, there is no tie upon us for not availing ourselves of a good offer.

In consequence of the unsettled state of affairs in the FRENCH WEST INDIES, and the apprehensions which timid minds are apt to entertain where there is only the appearance of danger, Stocks fell yesterday 1 per Cent, though at the close of the market they recovered a little. The rumour was that five men of war were to be immediately commissioned and sent to the West Indies.

William Pitt on Abolition

Despite the equation of abolitionism with Jacobinism, Wilberforce, on 2 April 1792, moved: '. . . that the trade carried on by British subjects for obtaining slaves on the coast of Africa ought to be abolished.' The House divided on an amendment to insert the word 'gradually' into the motion. This emasculating amendment was carried, even though Pitt, speaking at dawn after a tense night of debate, called for immediate abolition in one of the greatest anti-slavery speeches ever heard in Parliament.

. . . The point now in dispute between us is a difference *merely as to the period of time*, at which the Abolition of the Slave Trade ought to take place. I therefore congratulate this House, the Country and the World, that this great point is gained; that we may now consider this trade as *having received its condemnation*; that its *sentence is sealed*; that this *Curse of Mankind* is seen by the House in its true light; and that the greatest stigma on our national character which ever yet existed, is about to be removed! And, Sir (which is still more important), that MANKIND, I trust, *in general, are now likely to be delivered from the greatest practical evil that ever has afflicted the human race—from the severest and most extensive calamity recorded in the History of the World!* . . .

Why ought the Slave Trade to be abolished? BECAUSE IT IS AN INCURABLE INJUSTICE. How much stronger then is the argument for immediate, than gradual abolition! By allowing it to continue even for one hour, do not my Right Honourable Friends weaken,—do not they desert, their own argument of its injustice? If on the grounds of injustice it ought to be abolished at last, why ought it not now? . . . it is evident that there is a general conviction entertained of its being far from just, and from that very conviction of its injustice, some men have been led, I fear, to the supposition, that the Slave Trade never could have been permitted to begin, but from some strong and irresistible necessity; a necessity, however, which if it was fancied to exist at first . . . cannot be thought by any man whatever to exist now . . .

I know of no evil that ever has existed, nor can imagine one to exist, worse than the tearing of SEVENTY OR EIGHTY THOUSAND PERSONS *annually from their native land, by a combination of the civilised nations, inhabiting the most enlightened quarter of the globe; but more especially under the sanction of the laws of that nation, which calls herself the most free and the most happy of them all.* Even if these miserable beings were proved guilty of every crime before you take them off, of which however not a single proof is adduced, ought *we* to take upon ourselves the office of executioners? . . .

But if we go much further,—if we ourselves *tempt* them to sell their fellow-creatures to us, we may

rest assured, that they will take care to provide by every method, by kidnapping, by village-breaking, by unjust wars, by iniquitous condemnations, by rendering Africa a scene of bloodshed and misery, a supply of victims increasing in proportion to our demand.—Can we then hesitate in deciding whether the wars in Africa are their wars or ours? . . .

. . . Think of EIGHTY THOUSAND persons carried away out of their country by *we know not what means*! For crimes imputed! For light or inconsiderable faults! For debt perhaps! For the crime of witchcraft! Or a thousand other weak and scandalous pretexts! . . . There is something in the horror of it, that surpasses all the bounds of imagination. Admitting that there exists in Africa something like to Courts of Justice; yet what an office of humiliation and meanness is it in us, to take upon ourselves to carry into execution the partial, the cruel, iniquitous sentences of such Courts, as if we also were strangers to all religion, and to the first principles of justice . . . But the evil does not stop here . . . Do you think nothing of the ruin and the miseries in which so many other individuals, still remaining in Africa, are involved in consequence of carrying off so many myriads of people? Do you think nothing of their families which are left behind? . . . Do you think nothing of the miseries in consequence, that are felt from generation to generation? . . . Instead of any fair interchange of commodities; instead of conveying to them from this highly favoured land, any means of improvement, you carry with you that noxious plant by which every thing is withered and blasted; under whose shade nothing that is useful or profitable to Africa will ever flourish or take root . . . Africa is known to you only in its skirts. Yet even there you are able to infuse a poison that spreads its contagious effects from one end of it to the other, which penetrates to its very centre . . .

You are not sure, it is said, that other nations will give up this trade, if you should renounce it. I answer, if this trade . . . has in it a thousandth part of the criminality which I, and others, after thorough investigation of the subject, charge upon it; GOD forbid that we should hesitate in determining to relinquish so iniquitous a traffic; even though it should be retained by other countries, GOD forbid, however, that we should fail to do our utmost towards inducing other countries to abandon a bloody commerce which they have probably been in good measure led by our example to pursue . . .

. . . there is no nation in Europe that has, on the one hand, plunged so deeply into this guilt as Britain, or that is so likely, on the other, to be looked up to as an example, if she should have the manliness to be the first in decidedly renouncing it . . .

[Just as] *we* are now disposed to proscribe Africa [as incurably barbaric] . . . *we ourselves* might, in like manner, have been proscribed and forever shut out from all the blessings which we now enjoy . . .

Slaves, as we may read in Henry's History of Great Britain, were formerly an *established article of* OUR *exports*. "Great numbers," he says, "were exported like cattle, from the British coast, and were to be seen exposed for sale in the Roman market." . . . the historian tells you that "adultery, *witchcraft* and debt were probably some of the chief sources of supplying the Roman market with British Slaves"— that prisoners taken in war were added to the number . . . Every one of these sources of slavery has been stated . . . to be at this hour a source of slavery in Africa . . .

. . . Why might not some Roman Senator, reasoning on the principles of some Honourable Gentlemen, and pointing to *British barbarians*, have predicted with equal boldness, "*There* is a people that will never rise to civilisation—*there* is a people destined never to be free—a people without the

44 *Prime Minister William Pitt the Younger (1759-1806), friend of Wilberforce. An abolitionist, he shelved the cause temporarily during the war against Napoleon*

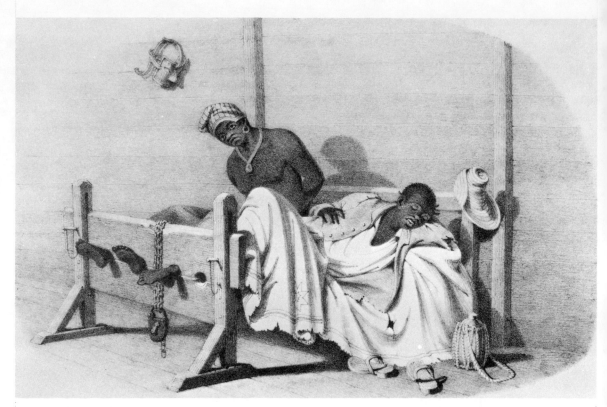

45, 46 *Stocks were standard punishment on plantations. Bed stocks* (above) *were usually used for drunkenness; standing stocks* (opposite), *for more serious transgressions*

continued. Items from THE ROYAL GAZETTE *of Kingston, Jamaica, record everyday events in the slaving colony.*

understanding necessary for the attainment of useful arts; depressed by the hand of nature below the level of the human species; and created to form a supply of Slaves for the rest of the world.".. .

.. . I shall .. . oppose to the utmost every proposition, which in any way may tend either to prevent, or even to postpone for an hour, the total Abolition of the Slave Trade .. .

Sale Notice for Slaves
Far away in the Sugar Islands the harsh repressions

Kingston, June 20, 1792
FOR SALE
on WEDNESDAY, the 27th inst.
520 Prime Gold-Coast NEGROES
Imported in the ship HERO, Capt. Quarrier
Allan, White & Co.

Kingston, June 15, 1792.
RAN AWAY from Hopewell Mountain, on the 13th instant a young negro wench, named NELLY, about 5 feet 5 inches high, and about 23 years old, of a

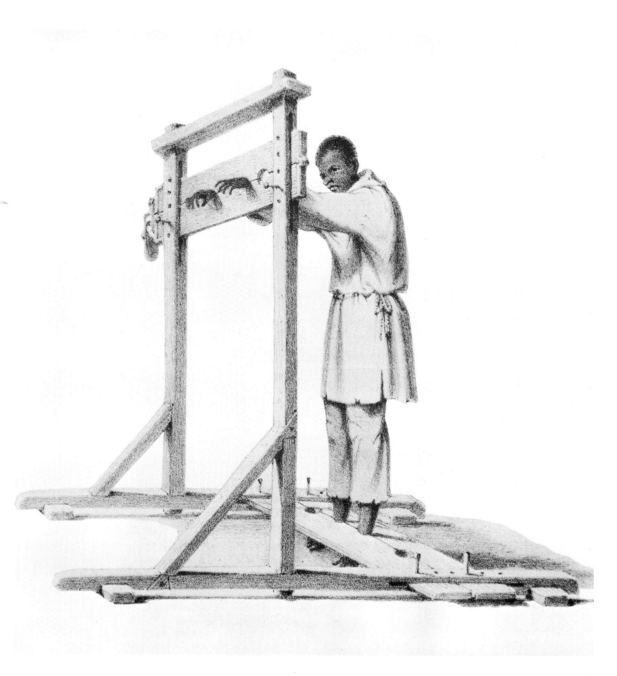

TO BE SOLD & LET

BY PUBLIC AUCTION,

On MONDAY the 18th of MAY, 1829,

UNDER THE TREES.

FOR SALE,

THE THREE FOLLOWING

SLAVES,

VIZ.

HANNIBAL, about 30 Years old, an excellent House Servant, of Good Character.
WILLIAM, about 35 Years old, a Labourer.
NANCY, an excellent House Servant and Nurse.

The MEN belonging to "LEECH'S" Estate, and the WOMAN to Mrs. D. SMIT

TO BE LET,

On the usual conditions of the Hirer finding them in Food, Clothing, and Medical Attendance,

THE FOLLOWING

MALE and FEMALE

SLAVES,

OF GOOD CHARACTERS,

ROBERT BAGLEY, about 20 Years old, a good House Servant.
WILLIAM BAGLEY, about 18 Years old, a Labourer.
JOHN ARMS, about 18 Years old.
JACK ANTONIA, about 40 Years old, a Labourer.
PHILIP, an Excellent Fisherman.
HARRY, about 27 Years old, a good House Servant.
LUCY, a Young Woman of good Character, used to House Work and the Nursery.
ELIZA, an Excellent Washerwoman.
CLARA, an Excellent Washerwoman.
FANNY, about 14 Years old, House Servant.
SARAH, about 14 Years old, House Servant.

Also for Sale, at Eleven o'Clock,

Fine Rice, Gram, Paddy, Books, Muslins, Needles, Pins, Ribbons, &c. &c.

AT ONE O'CLOCK, THAT CELEBRATED ENGLISH HORSE

BLUCHER,

yellowish complexion, a Chamba; she is a field negro, talks little or no English, and has three scars on each side of her face. Any person who can give information, so that she may be found, or will deliver her at the above Mountain, lodge her in any of the workhouses; or bring her to the Subscriber, shall receive twenty shillings reward.

JAMES WELSH

Parliament Abolishes the Slave Trade

Year after year Wilberforce raised the abolition issue in the House, only to be rejected. War with France had erupted, and many saw his cause as tantamount to treason. Britain's slave trade, far from being eradicated, grew to unprecedented heights. By 1800 Liverpool had ninety per cent of the world's African commerce, with profits reaching 30 per cent. But as the war dragged on, Bonaparte, rather than French Jacobinism, became the enemy, and the treason charge lost force.

At the same time, with European ports closed to English sugar, the planters, facing collapsing markets, sank slowly and irretrievably into debt. Moreover, generations of intensive cultivation had impoverished the islands' soil. For these and related reasons, Wilberforce, in 1804, after four years of diminishing hope, during which he had not even brought the matter up, renewed his efforts.

But it was not until 1807 that the convergent pressures of humanitarianism and finance at last proved strong enough to bring the traffic, though not slavery itself, to an end. The bill which outlawed British participation in the trade was intrpduced in the House of Lords on 5 February 1807 by Lord Grenville, who had become prime minister following Pitt's death the year before. It was brought into the House of Commons five days later by the Foreign Secretary,

47 *Trained negroes in the West Indies were not only sold, but rented out at a profit during slack seasons when their owners could spare them*

Charles Grey, Lord Hawick. It received the royal assent on 25 March.

Whereas the Two Houses of Parliament did, by their Resolutions of the Tenth and Twenty-fourth Days of June One thousand eight hundred and six, severally resolve, upon certain Grounds therein mentioned, that they would, with all practicable Expedition, take effectual Measures for the Abolition of the African Slave Trade, in such Manner, and at such Period as might be deemed adviseable: And Whereas it is fit upon all and each of the Grounds mentioned in the said Resolutions, that the same should be forthwith abolished and prohibited, and declared to be unlawful; be it therefore enacted . . . That from and after the First Day of May One thousand eight hundred and seven, the African Slave Trade, and all and all manner of dealing and trading in the Purchase, Sale, Barter, or Transfer of Slaves, or of Persons intended to be sold, transferred, used, or dealt with as Slaves, practiced and carried on, in, at, to or from any Part of the Coast or Countries of Africa, shall be, and the same is hereby utterly abolished, prohibited, and declared to be unlawful; and also that all and all manner of dealing, either by way of Purchase, Sale, Barter, or Transfer, or by means of any other Contract or Agreement whatever, relating to any Slaves, or to any Persons intended to be used or dealt with as Slaves, for the Purpose of such Slaves or Persons being removed and transported either immediately or by Transhipment at Sea or otherwise, directly or indirectly from Africa, or from any Island, Country, Territory, or Place whatever, in the West Indies, or in any other Part of America, not being in the Dominion, Possession, or Occupation of His Majesty, to any other Island, Country, Territory or Place whatever, is hereby in like Manner utterly abolished, prohibited, and declared to be unlawful; and if any of His Majesty's Subjects, or any Person or Persons resident

Within the image (engraving text):
Pub.d April 28, 1791 by H. Humphrey N.18. Old Bond Street

BARBARITIES in the WEST INDIAS

Mr Frances relates "Amongst numberless other acts of Cruelty daily practised, an English Negro Driver, because a young Negro thro' Sickness was unable to work, threw him into a Copper of boiling Sugar Juice, & after keeping him staved over head & Ears for above Three Quarters of an hour in the boiling liquid, whipt him with such severity, that it was near Six Months before he recovered of his Wounds & Scalding."
Vide Mr Frances sketch, corroborated by Mr Fox Mr Wilberforce & &c

48, 49 *Cartoonists clashed in the propaganda battle. Anti-slavers circulated the print (above), said to be based on fact, of a slave cast into a cauldron of boiling sugar. Pro-slavers caricatured pious abolitionists (opposite) as dallying with negro women*

within this United Kingdom, or any of the Islands, Colonies, Dominions, or Territories thereto belonging, or in His Majesty's Occupation or Possession, shall from and after the Day aforesaid, by him or themselves, or by his or their Factors or Agents or otherwise howsoever, deal or trade in, purchase, sell, barter, or transfer, or contract or agree for the dealing or trading in, purchasing, selling, bartering, or transferring of any Slave or Slaves, or any Person or Persons intended to be sold, transferred, used, or dealt with as a Slave or Slaves contrary to the Prohibitions of this Act, he or they so offending shall forfeit and pay for every such Offence the Sum of

One hundred Pounds of lawful Money of Great Britain for each and every Slave so purchased, sold, bartered, or transferred, or contracted or agreed for as aforesaid, the One Moiety thereof to the Use of His Majesty, His Heirs and Successors, and the other Moiety to the Use of any Person who shall inform, sue, and prosecute for the same . . .

CHAPTER FIVE

The Torment Ends (1816-65)

The Anti-Slavery Patrol

The United States, in the year that Britain banned the trade (1807), had also attempted to end it by outlawing the importation of negroes. But so great was the demand for slaves in the cotton-growing states, and so available were men daring enough to smuggle where they could not legally import, that congressional abolition was a dead letter from the start. The illicit trade became bigger and more prosperous than the legal trade had ever been.

Although the two nations later agreed to police the seas jointly to thwart the contraband traffic, few American warships were sent on station. Moreover, Washington refused to permit foreign powers to stop and search vessels flying the American flag, thus offering an umbrella of protection to the smugglers.

For nearly sixty years, Royal Navy vessels, strung out thinly along 2,000 miles of the West African coast, bore the brunt of the anti-slavery patrol. Tours of duty in the steaming heat lasted months. The ships prowled malaria-ridden backwaters, their wooden hulls crawling with giant cockroaches, their sun-baked guns scorching to the touch. The following INSTRUCTIONS, issued to a patrol commander in 1816, suggest the gruelling nature of the task.

Admiralty Office,
Whitehall

You are hereby required and directed to put to sea, in the ship you command, as soon as she shall in all respects be ready to sail, and proceed without delay to the coast of Africa, for the purpose of visiting the several British forts and settlements on that coast and rendering them such assistance and protection as you may find them to require.

You are to repair in the first instance to Sierra Leone . . . In proceeding down the coast you are diligently to look into the several bays and creeks on the same between Cape de Verd and Benguela, particularly on the Gold Coast, Whydah, the Bight of

Benin, and Angola, in order to your seizing such ships or vessels as may be liable thereto, under the authority of the several Acts of Parliament prohibiting the slave trade (abstracts or copies of which we herewith inclose for your information and guidance); and you are to use every other means in your power to prevent a continuance of the traffic in slaves and to give full effect to the Acts of Parliament in question . . .

    Given under our hands the 20th March 1816

J. S. Yorke
Geo. Haye
B. P. Blackford
BY ORDER J. W. Croker

Sir James Lucas Yeo, KCB,
Captain of His Majesty's ship
the *Inconstant*.

The Testimony of Slaves in Court

Although the tide of abolitionism was now almost at the full in much of the English-speaking world, the status of the negro remained, in many eyes, on a sub-human level, without credibility and without dignity. Most West Indian judges, for example, refused to accept the sworn evidence of blacks in court. An exchange of correspondence on the subject of the negro's position in the Sugar Islands appeared in the London GLOBE AND TRAVELLER *in 1823, during which this letter, dated 9 December, from a Mr John Foster appeared.*

Much has been said about the evidence of negroes not being admitted in courts of justice. It were to be wished that they were in a situation to give credible

50 *HMS* Brisk, *of the Royal Navy's anti-slavery patrol, attacks an illegal slaver,* The Sunny South. *Captured ships were seized, their living cargoes returned to Africa and freed*

evidence, but they are without any defined religion, those, comparatively few excepted, who have been converted to Christianity . . .

A Jew may swear by the Old Testament; a Quaker's affirmation may be believed. A Mohammedan may perhaps be believed upon his Koran. But a heathenish negro must swear by his *Obeahs*, or by the little idols that stand on his chimney piece. To what absurdities would emancipators lead us!

An American Negro on English Attitudes

Shortly before the outlawing of slavery under the British flag, a group of refugee negroes who had founded a settlement in Ontario, Canada, and named it Wilberforce, sent one of their number, the Rev Nathaniel Paul, to England. His mission was to raise money and to lecture against American slavery. Many of his fellow-refugees had been forced to flee twice—first from the South to Cincinnati, Ohio, and when harassed there as well, on into Canada. On 10 April 1833, Paul wrote from Bristol to the American abolitionist, William Lloyd Garrison, giving a sharply-observed picture of English behaviour towards the blacks at that crucial time.

. . . I have been engaged, for several months past, in travelling through the country and delivering lectures upon the system of slavery as it exists in the United States . . . My lectures have been numerously attended by from two to three thousand people, the

51 *Slaves picking cotton in the southern United States. The crop was known as 'King Cotton' because it was the supreme cash-earner. Secondary crops were tobacco and rice*

52 *Ceremony in Guiana, 1838, to commemorate anniversary of the freeing of field labourers. Although former slaves here appear prosperous, others, as in all colonies after emancipation, became vagrants or criminals*

Halls and Chapels have been overflowing . . . I have not failed to give Uncle Sam due credit for his 2,000,000 slaves; nor to expose the cruel prejudices of the Americans to our colored race . . . to the astonishment of the people here. And is this, they say, republican liberty? God deliver us from it.

And now, to contrast the difference in the treatment that a colored man receives in this country, with that which he receives in America, my soul is filled with sorrow and indignation. I could weep over the land of my nativity! . . . Here, if I go to church, I am not pointed to the "Negro seat" in the gallery; but any gentleman opens his pew door for my reception. If I wish for a passage in a stage, the only question that is asked me is, "Which do you choose, sir, an inside or an outside seat?" If I

stop at a public inn, no one would ever think here of setting a separate table for me; I am conducted to the same table with other gentlemen. The only difference that I have ever discovered is this, I am generally taken for a stranger, and they therefore seem anxious to pay me the greater respect.

I have had the pleasure of breakfasting twice with the venerable Wilberforce, and have now a letter in my pocket that I received from him, a few weeks since, which I would not take pounds for. Once I have been in the company of the patriotic Clarkson. I must say I view them both as Angels of Liberty. God bless and reward them . . .

England Abolishes Slavery
Wilberforce was by then tired and spent. In July, as Parliament debated the measure which was finally to end slavery, he lay dying. The BILL *became law on 28 August 1833, one month after his death.*

89

ANNO TERTIO & QUARTO
GULIELMI IV. REGIS.

C A P. LXXIII.

An Act for the Abolition of Slavery throughout the *British* Colonies; for promoting the Industry of the manumitted Slaves; and for compensating the Persons hitherto entitled to the Services of such Slaves.

WHEREAS divers Persons are holden in Slavery within divers of His Majesty's Colonies, and it is just and expedient that all such Persons should be manumitted and set free, and that a reasonable Compensation should be made to the Persons hitherto entitled to the Services of such Slaves for the Loss which they will incur by being deprived of the Right to such Services: And whereas it is also expedient that Provision should be made for promoting the Industry and securing the good Conduct of the Persons so to be manumitted, for a limited Period after such their Manumission: And whereas it is necessary that the Laws now in force in the said several Colonies should forthwith be adapted to the new State and Relations of Society therein which will follow upon such general Manumission as aforesaid of the said Slaves; and that, in order to afford the necessary Time for such Adaptation of the said Laws, a short Interval should elapse before such Manumission should take effect: Be it therefore enacted by the King's most Excellent Majesty, by and with the Advice and Consent of the Lords Spiritual and Temporal, and Commons, in this present Parliament assembled, and by the Authority of the same, That from and after the First Day of *August* One thousand eight hundred and thirty-four all Persons who in conformity with the Laws now in force in the said Colonies respectively shall on or before the [said day] . . . have been duly registered as Slaves in any such Colony, and . . . be actually within any such Colony, and who shall by such Registries appear to be . . . of the full Age of Six Years or upwards, shall by force and virtue of this Act, and without the previous Execution of any Indenture of Apprenticeship, or other Deed or Instrument for that Purpose, become and be apprenticed Labourers; provided that, for the Purposes aforesaid, every Slave engaged in his ordinary Occupation on the Seas shall be deemed and taken to be within the Colony to which such Slaves shall belong.

The Act specified that field labourers were to serve as indentured apprentices for six years after its passage, and slaves otherwise employed for four. In fact, the whole apprenticeship idea was scuttled as unworkable by the planters themselves long before the time ran out. The Act also provided for the labourers to be fed, clothed and housed; and given plots of land to cultivate for their own benefit. They were to work only forty-five hours a week; were not to work on Sunday; were not to be prevented from attending church, and not to be whipped.

Parliament set aside £20 million to compensate their owners, individual payments to be calculated upon the average slave price in each of the colonial territories over the years 1822–30. The dying Wilberforce commented, 'Thank God that I should have lived to see the day in which England is willing to give twenty millions sterling for the abolition of slavery.'

The TWELFTH CLAUSE *contained these unequivocal words:*

. . . And be it further enacted, That, subject to the Obligations imposed by this Act, or to be imposed by any such Act of General Assembly, Ordinance, or Order in Council as herein-after mentioned, upon such apprentice Labourers as aforesaid, all and every the Persons who on this said First Day of *August* One thousand eight hundred and thirty-four shall be holden in Slavery within any such *British* Colony as aforesaid shall upon and from and after the [said day] . . . become and be to all Intents and Purposes

53 *Freed slaves aboard a Royal Navy vessel remove their shackles. The patrol operated from 1808 until 1867. Every slave liberated by the English spurred the American negroes' fight for liberty*

free and discharged of and from all Manner of Slavery, and shall be absolutely and for ever manumitted; and that the Children thereafter to be born to any such Persons, and the Offspring of such Children, shall in like Manner be free from their Birth; and that from and after the [said day] . . . Slavery shall be and is hereby utterly and for ever abolished and declared unlawful throughout the *British* Colonies, Plantations, and Possessions Abroad . . .

The Repression of American Slaves

Emancipation by the British was a trumpet call to American slaves, thousands of whom clamoured for, fought for and escaped to freedom. But the slavery issue in the United States was far more complex and had both subtler and more immediate implications than in Britain, where the concern was with colonies thousands of miles from home.

In the United States, slavery was not merely on the doorstep; it was within the house, poisoning the atmosphere. It affected politics on every level. It affected the status of the new territories to the west and their admission into the union. It affected everyday commercial dealings between southern plantation-owners and northern financiers and manufacturers; many of the northerners, although philosophically pro-freedom, opposed emancipation on business grounds.

Slaughter and pillage by the blacks brought intensified cruelty and repression by the whites. The famous rebellion of 1831 in Southampton County, Virginia, led by Nat Turner, a slave and religious mystic who could read and write, terrified the entire South. It took a combination of state and federal troops to crush it. Afterwards, a Virginia legislator commented:

'We have, as far as possible, closed every avenue by which light might enter their minds. If you could extinguish the capacity to see the light, our work would be completed; they would then be on a level with the beasts of the field, and we should be safe . . .'

In all southern states, the law and the church conspired to 'keep the nigras in their place'. To give them formal education, even in religious matters, was a crime. In Norfolk, Virginia, in 1853, a teacher, Mrs Douglas, was sentenced for 'assembling with negroes to instruct them to read and write'. The judge:

. . . There are persons, I believe, in our community . . . [who] profess to believe that universal intellectual culture is necessary to religious instruction and education, and that such culture is suitable to a state of slavery; and there can be no misapprehension as to your opinions on this subject, judging from the indiscreet freedom with which you spoke of your regard for the colored race in general. Such opinions in the present state of our society I regard as manifestly mischievous. It is not true that our slaves cannot be taught religious and moral duty, without being able to read the Bible and use the pen . . .

A valuable report . . . by the Southern Aid Society . . . shows that a system of catechetical instruction with a clear and simple exposition of Scripture, has been employed with gratifying success; that the slave population of the South are peculiarly susceptible of good religious influences. Their mere residence among a Christian people has wrought a great and happy change in their condition: they have been raised from the night of heathenism to the light of Christianity . . .

Of the one hundred millions of the negro race, there cannot be found another so large a body as the three millions of slaves in the United States, at once so intelligent, so inclined to the Gospel, and so blessed by the elevating influence of civilization and Christianity. Occasional instances of cruelty and oppression, it is true, may sometimes occur, and probably will ever continue to take place under any system of laws; but this is not confined to wrongs committed upon the negro; wrongs are committed and cruelly practiced in a like degree by the lawless

54 *Cincinnati on the Ohio River, one of the important Union cities which received runaway blacks from the South. The founders of Wilberforce, Canada, made their way north from Cincinnati*

white man upon his own color; and while the negroes of our town and State are known to be surrounded by most of the substantial comforts of life, and invited both by precept and example to participate in proper, moral and religious duties, it argues, it seems to me, a sickly sensibility towards them to say their persons and feelings, and interests are not sufficiently respected by our laws . . .

. . . the first legislative provision upon this subject was introduced in the year 1831, immediately succeeding the bloody scenes of the memorable Southampton insurrection; and that law being found not sufficiently penal to check the wrongs complained of, was re-enacted with additional penalties in the year 1848 . . . After these several and repeated recognitions of the wisdom and propriety of the said act, it may well be said that bold and open opposition to it is a matter not to be slightly regarded...

There might have been no occasion for such enactments in Virginia, or elsewhere, on the subject of negroe education, but as a matter of self-defense against the schemes of Northern incendiaries, and the outcry against holding our slaves in bondage. Many now living well remember how, and when, and why the anti-slavery fury began ... Our mails were clogged with abolition pamphlets and inflammatory documents, to be distributed among our Southern negroes to induce them to cut our throats ... These, however, were not the only means resorted to by the Northern fanatics to stir up insubordination among our slaves. They scattered far and near pocket handkerchiefs, and other similar articles, with frightful engravings, and printed over with anti-slavery nonsense, with a view to work upon the feeling and ignorance of our negroes, who otherwise would have remained comfortable and happy ... In vindication of the policy and justice of our laws, which every individual should be taught to respect, the judgment of the Court is, in addition to the proper fine and costs, that you be imprisoned for the period of one month in the jail of this city ...

Bishop Meade of Virginia composed a cautionary SERMON *for slave congregations on plantations, which was published in 1856.*

... Having thus shown you the chief duties you owe to your great Master in heaven, I now come to lay before you the duties you owe to your masters and mistresses here upon earth. And for this you have

55 *A slave sale in Virginia just before the Civil War. Although the auctioneer appears to be selling this family as a single lot, families were often split among various owners*

NOTICE

NEGROES
FOR SALE
AT AUCTION
TH'S DAY
AT 1 O'CLOCK

THE NEW YORK HERALD

95.

one general rule, that you ought always to carry in your minds; and that is to do all service for them as if you did it for God himself.

Poor creatures! you little consider, when you are idle and neglectful of your masters' business, when you steal, and waste, and hurt any of their substance, when you are saucy and impudent, when you are telling them lies and deceiving them . . . you do not consider, I say, that what faults you are guilty of towards your masters and mistresses are faults done against God himself, who hath set your masters and mistresses over you in his own stead, and expects that you would do for them just as you would do for him . . . your masters and mistresses are God's overseers, and . . . if you are faulty towards them, God himself will punish you severely for it in the next world . . .

The Underground Railroad

In the lore of American slavery, the so-called Underground Railroad bulks large. Historically, it had its model in the rescue operations mounted during the French revolution for the extrication of those proscribed by the Terror. The fictional deeds of Baroness Orczy's Scarlet Pimpernel saw parallels time and again in those of agents of the Underground Railroad.

The negro rescue system consisted of a series of secret 'stations' whose agents would pass a fugitive along from one to the next, until at last he reached safety. There were numerous 'lines' via the southern border states to the free North and Canada.

The Railroad began in the 1820s. It reached its peak during the tense period of John Brown's raid on Harper's Ferry, Virginia (1859), and continued well into the Civil War.

Renowned white abolitionists worked closely with the Railroad, as did many free negroes, including William Still, the 'stationmaster' at the strategic junction of Philadelphia. THREE LETTERS *to Still:*

[13 June 1858, Camden, Maryland]
Mr. Still: —I writ to inform you that we stand in need of help if ever we wonted help it is in theas day, we have Bin trying to rais money to By a hors but there is so few here that we can trust our selves with . . . i wont to no if your friends can help us, we have a Road that more than 100 past over in 1857 . . . there is no better in the State, we are 7 miles from Delaware Bay. you may understand what i mean. I wrote last december to the anti Slavery Society for James Mot and others concerning of purchasing a horse for this Bisnes if your friends can help us the work must stil go on for there is much frait pases over this Road, But ther has Ben but 3 conductors for sum time. you may no that there is but few men, sum talks all dos nothing, there is horses owned by Collard peopel but not for this purpose. We wont one for to go when called for, one of our best men was nigh Cut By keeping of them too long, By not having means to convay them tha must Be convad if they pass over this Road safe tha go through in 2 nights to Wilmington, for i went there with 28 in one gang last November, tha had to ride for when thea com to us we go 15 miles, it is hard Road to travel . . . pleas try what you can do for us this is the place we need help, 12 mile i live from mason and Dixson Line. I wod have come but cant have time, as yet there has been some fuss about a boy ho lived near Camden, he has gone away, he ses me and my brother nose about it but he dont . . .

. . . Ancer this letter.

Pleas to writ let me no if you can do anything for us. I still remain your friend.

[16 April 1859, Baltimore, Maryland]
Dear Brother i have taken the opportunity of writing you these few lines to inform you that i am well an hoping these few lines may find you enjoying the same good blessing please to write me word at what

THE OLD PLANTATION HOME.

56 *An idealised 'Uncle Tom's cabin' in the American South, the occupants revelling near the owner's 'big house'. Such popular depictions ignored the cruel aspects of plantation life*

57 *Runaway slaves often entered the Union Army's lines and did menial work for the troops. They were known as 'contrabands'*

time was it when israel went to Jericho i am very anxious to hear for thare is a mighty host will pass over and you and i my brother will sing hally luja i shall notify you when the great catastrophe shal take place No more at the present but remain your brother

N.L.J.

[17 October 1860, Petersburg, Virginia]
Dear Sir . . . I feel as much determined to work in this glorious cause, as ever I did in all of my life, and I have some very good hams on hand that I would like very much for you to have. I have nothing of interest to write about just now, only that the politics of the day is in a high rage, and I don't know of the result, therefore, I want you to be one of those wide-a-wakes as is mentioned from your section of country now-a-days, &c. Also, if you wish to write to me, Mr. J. Brown will inform you how

to direct a letter to me.

No more at present, until I hear from you; but I want you to be a wide-awake.

Yours in haste,

HAM & EGGS

A Runaway Slave

Surrounded by white freedom, the slave existed as a small black island of imprisonment. His eagerness to escape into that freedom, despite danger and hardship, was incomprehensible to many owners, as indicated in this LETTER *dated 20 February 1860 from Mrs Sarah Logue, of Bigbyville, Tennessee to her former slave, the Rev J. W. Loguen of Syracuse, New York.*

To Jarm:—I now take my pen to write you a few lines, to let you know how we all are. I am a cripple, but I am still able to get about. The rest of the family are all well. Cherry is as well as common. I write you these lines to let you know the situation we are in,—partly in consequence of your running away and stealing Old Rock, our fine mare. Though we got the mare back, she never was worth much after you took her;—and, as I now stand in need of some funds, I have determined to sell you, and I have had an offer for you, but did not see fit to take it. If you will send me one thousand dollars, and pay for the old mare, I will give up all claim I have to you . . . In consequence of your running away, we had to sell Abe and Ann and twelve acres of land; and I want you to send me the money, that I may be able to redeem the land . . . If you do not comply with my request, I will sell you to some one else, and you may rest assured that the time is not far distant when things will be changed with you . . .

I understand that you are a preacher. As the Southern people are so bad you had better come and preach to your old acquaintances. I would like to know if you read your Bible. If so, can you tell me what will become of the thief if he does not repent?

. . . You know that we reared you as we reared our own children; that you was never abused, and that shortly before you ran away, when your master asked if you would like to be sold, you said you would not leave him to go with anybody.

[From the Rev J. W. Loguen, 28 March 1860]
Mrs. Sarah Logue: Yours of the 20th of February is duly received, and I thank you for it. It is a long time since I heard from my poor old mother, and I am glad to know that she is yet alive, and, as you say, "as well as common." What that means, I don't know. I wish you had said more about her.

You are a woman; but, had you a woman's heart, you never could have insulted a brother by telling him you sold his only remaining brother and sister, because he put himself beyond your power to convert him into money.

. . . Now you have the unutterable meanness to ask me to return and be your miserable chattel, or in lieu thereof, send you $1000 to enable you to redeem the *land*, but not to redeem my poor brother and sister! If I were to send you money, it would be to get my brother and sister, and not that you should get land. You say you are a *cripple*, and doubtless you say it to stir my pity, for you knew I was susceptible in that direction. I do pity you from the bottom of my heart. Nevertheless, I am indignant beyond the power of words to express, that you should be so sunken and cruel as to tear the hearts I love so much all in pieces; that you should be willing to impale and crucify us all, out of compassion for your poor *foot* or *leg*. Wretched woman! be it known to you that I value my freedom, to say nothing of my mother, brothers and sisters, more than your whole body; more, indeed, than my own life; more than all the lives of all the slaveholders and tyrants under heaven.

. . . you say, "You know we raised you as we did our own children." Woman, did you raise your *own children* for the market? Did you raise them for the whipping-post? Did you raise them to be driven off, bound to a coffle in chains? Where are my poor bleeding brothers and sisters? Can you tell? Who was it that sent them off into sugar and cotton fields, to be kicked and cuffed, and whipped, and to groan and die; and where no kin can hear their groans, or attend and sympathize at their dying bed, or follow in their funeral? Wretched woman! Do you say *you* did not do it? Then I reply, your husband did, and *you* approved the deed—and the very letter you sent me shows that your heart approves it all. Shame on you! . . .

But you say I am a thief, because I took the old mare along with me. Have you got to learn that I had a better right to the old mare, as you call her, than Mannasseth Logue had to me? Is it a greater sin for me to steal his horse, than it was for him to rob my mother's cradle, and steal me? . . . Before God and high heaven, is there a law for one man which is not a law for every other man?

If you or any other speculator on my body and rights, wish to know how I regard my rights, they need but come here, and lay their hands on me to enslave me. Did you think to terrify me by presenting the alternatives to give my money to you, or give my body to slavery? Then let me say to you, that I meet the proposition with unutterable scorn and contempt . . . I stand among a free people, who, I thank God, sympathize with my rights, and the rights of mankind; and if your emissaries and venders come here to re-enslave me, and escape the unshrinking vigor of my own right arm, I trust my strong and brave friends, in this city and State, will be my rescuers and avengers.

Negro Volunteers for the Civil War

When the Civil War broke out, many southern negroes escaped and took refuge in the Union lines, where they were put to work in menial jobs, as teamsters, labourers and so on. They were known as 'contrabands'. At the same time, many free northern negroes offered to serve as Union soldiers. These were at first rejected. President Abraham Lincoln's policy was the preservation of the Union, and not the alienation of the southern states: the Confederate rebels would have been personally affronted had they been forced to face negro troops in battle, and, it was feared, would therefore fight all the harder.

Washington, April 23d, 1861

Hon. Simon Cameron,
Secretary of War
Sir: I desire to inform you that I know of some three hundred of reliable colored free citizens of this City, who desire to enter the service for the defence of the City.

I have been three times across the Rocky Mountains in the service of the Country with Frémont and others.

I can be found about the Senate Chambers, as I have been employed about the premises for some years.

Yours respectfully,

Jacob Dodson
(Colored)

Secretary Cameron replied: 'I have to say that this Department has no intention at present to call into the service of the government any colored soldiers.' A year later, however, the ban was removed; negroes were permitted to enlist, an expedient to compensate for heavy Union losses.

The Emancipation Proclamation
Although President Lincoln personally abhorred

58 *Abraham Lincoln (1809-65), Civil War president of the United States and author of the Emancipation Proclamation*

59 *Company E, 4th US Colored Infantry, free negroes who joined the Union Army to fight the Confederacy in the Civil War*

slavery, he was unwilling to take any steps towards emancipation until the strength of the Confederate armies compelled him to do so as a military necessity. His famous Emancipation Proclamation of 1 January 1863 did not, in practical terms, set a single slave free. Those to whom it applied were resident in the rebellious states where the promulgation, naturally enough, was ignored; it did, however, serve as a rallying cry for the negroes themselves. Slaves in territories either not in revolt or which had already been reconquered remained unaffected.

Whereas on the 22d day of September, A.D. 1862, a proclamation was issued by the President of the United States, containing among other things, the following, to wit:

"That on the 1st day of January, A.D. 1863, all persons held as slaves within any State or designated part of a State the people whereof shall then be in rebellion against the United States shall be then, thenceforward, and forever free; and the executive government of the United States, including the military and naval authority thereof, will recognize and maintain the freedom of such persons and will do no act or acts to repress such persons, or any of them, in any efforts they may make for their actual freedom.

"That the executive will on the 1st day of January aforesaid, by proclamation, designate the States and parts of States, if any, in which the people thereof, respectively, shall then be in rebellion against the United States; and the fact that any State or the people thereof shall on that day be in good faith represented in the Congress of the United States by members chosen thereto at elections wherein a majority of the qualified voters of such States shall have participated shall, in the absence of strong countervailing testimony, be deemed conclusive evidence that such State and the people thereof are not then in rebellion against the United States."

Now, therefore, I, Abraham Lincoln, President of the United States, by virtue of the power in me vested as Commander-in-Chief of the Army and Navy of the United States in time of actual armed rebellion against the authority and government of the United States, and as a fit and necessary war measure for suppressing said rebellion, do, on this 1st day of January, A.D. 1863, and in accordance with my purpose so to do, publicly proclaimed for the full period of one hundred days from the first day above mentioned, order and designate as the States and parts of States wherein the people thereof, respectively, are this day in rebellion against the United States the following, to wit:

Arkansas, Texas, Louisiana (except the parishes of St. Bernard, Plaquemines, Jefferson, St. John, St. Charles, St. James, Ascension, Assumption, Terrebonne, Lafourche, St. Mary, St. Martin, and Orleans, including the city of New Orleans), Mississippi, Alabama, Florida, Georgia, South Carolina, North Carolina, and Virginia (except the forty-eight counties designated as West Virginia, and also the counties of Berkeley, Accomac, Northhampton, Elizabeth City, York, Princess Anne, and Norfolk, including the cities of Norfolk and Portsmouth), and which excepted parts are for the present left precisely as if this proclamation were not issued.

And by virtue of the power and for the purpose aforesaid, I do order and declare that all persons held as slaves within said designated States and parts of States are, and henceforward shall be, free; and that the Executive Government of the United States, including the military and naval authorities thereof, will recognize and maintain the freedom of said persons.

And I hereby enjoin upon the people so declared to be free to abstain from all violence, unless in necessary self-defense; and I recommend to them that, in all cases when allowed, they labor faithfully for reasonable wages.

And I further declare and make known that such persons of suitable condition will be received into the armed service of the United States to garrison forts, positions, stations, and other places, and to man vessels of all sorts in said service.

And upon this act, sincerely believed to be an act of justice, warranted by the Constitution upon military necessity, I invoke the considerate judgment of mankind and the gracious favor of Almighty God.

The Thirteenth Amendment
Slavery throughout the United States came to an end with the thirteenth amendment to the Constitution, passed during the incumbency of Lincoln's successor, President Andrew Johnson, and ratified in December 1865.

Resolved by the Senate and House of Representatives of the United States of America in Congress assembled (two-thirds of both Houses concurring) That the following article be proposed to the Legislatures of the several States as an amendment to the Constitution of the United States, which, when ratified by

60 *President Lincoln enters Richmond, Virginia, after its capture by Union forces, four days before the Confederacy's surrender. Freed slaves cheer their emancipator*

PROCLAMATION OF EMANCIPATION

"UPON THIS ACT, ... I INVOKE THE CONSIDERATE JUDGMENT OF MANKIND AND THE GRACIOUS FAVOR OF ALMIGHTY GOD."

A. LINCOLN

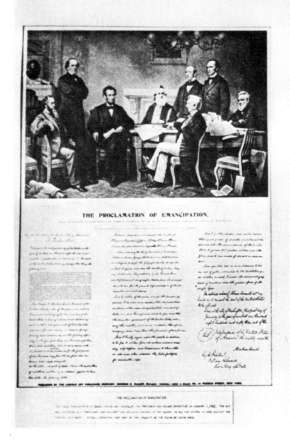

61 *Exhibited in the Lincoln Museum, Washington DC (left), a replica of the Emancipation Proclamation and an engraving of Lincoln reading the document to his cabinet. (Right) A replica of the Thirteenth Amendment to the Constitution*

three-quarters of such Legislatures, shall be valid, to all intents and purposes, as part of the said Constitution: namely,

Article XIII, Section 1. Neither slavery nor involuntary servitude, except as a punishment for crime whereof the party shall have been duly convicted, shall exist within the United States, or any place subject to their jurisdiction.

Section 2. Congress shall have power to enforce this Article by appropriate legislation.

The amendment was ratified by twenty-seven states, the requisite three-quarters of the thirty-six states then in the Union. The document concluded:

Now therefore be it known that I, William H. Seward, Secretary of State of the United States ... do hereby certify that the amendment aforesaid has become valid, to all intents and purposes, as a part of the Constitution of the United States.

Bibliography

APTHEKER, HERBERT. *A Documentary History of the Negro People in the United States*, The Citadel Press, New York, 1965

CATTERALL, HELEN TUNNICLIFF. *Judicial Cases Concerning American Slavery and the Negro* (vol I), Carnegie Institute, Washington, DC, 1926

COMMAGER, H. S. *Documents of American History*, Crofts American History Series, New York, 1934

COMMONS, HOUSE OF. *The Debate on a Motion for the Abolition of the Slave-Trade, in the House of Commons on Monday the Second of April, 1792, Reported in Detail*, Printed by W. Woodfall, and sold at the Printing-Office of the Diary, Salisbury-Square, Fleet-Street, London, 1792

COMMONS, HOUSE OF. *Minutes of the Evidence Delivered before a Select Committee of the Whole House to Whom it Was Referred to Consider of the Slave Trade*, Printed by Order of the House of Commons in *Parliamentary Papers*, 1731–1800

COUGHLAN, ROBERT, and THE EDITORS OF *Life*. *Tropical Africa*, Time-Life International (Nederland NV), 1963

COUPLAND, SIR REGINALD. *The British Anti-Slavery Movement*, Frank Cass & Co Ltd, London, 1964

COUPLAND, SIR REGINALD. *Wilberforce*, Oxford at the Clarendon Press, 1923

CUGOANO, OTTOBAH. *Thoughts and Sentiments on the Evil and Wicked Traffic of the Slavery and Commerce of the Human Species*, T. Becket, London, 1787

DAVIDSON, BASIL. *The African Past*, Universal Library/Grosset & Dunlap, New York, 1967

DAVIDSON, BASIL. *The African Slave Trade*, Atlantic Monthly Press/Little, Brown & Co, Boston, Mass, 1961

DAVIDSON, BASIL. *A History of West Africa*, Anchor Books/Doubleday & Co, Garden City, NY, 1966

DAVIS, DAVID BRION. *The Problem of Slavery in Western Culture*, Cornell University Press, Ithaca, NY, 1966

'DICKEY SAM'. *Liverpool and Slavery*, A. Bowker & Son, Liverpool, 1884

DONNAN, ELIZABETH. *Documents Illustrative of the History of the Slave Trade to America* (vols I, II, III), Carnegie Institute, Washington, DC, 1930, 1931, 1932

EDWARDS, BRYAN. *The History, Civil and Commercial, of the British Colonies in the West Indies*, J. Stockdale, London, 1801

ENFIELD, WILLIAM. *An Essay Towards the History of Liverpool*, Joseph Johnson, London, 1774

ENGLISH HISTORICAL DOCUMENTS. *1714–1783* (vol X), State Paper Room, British Museum

EQUIANO, OLAUDAH. *Equiano's Travels—His Autobiography* (Editor: Paul Edwards), Heinemann, London, 1967

FRANKLIN, JOHN HOPE. *From Slavery to Freedom*, Alfred A. Knopf, New York, 1966

Gentleman's Magazine and Historical Chronicle (vol X), 1740, and (vol LIII), 1783

GENOVESE, EUGENE D. *The Political Economy of the Slave Trade*, Pantheon Books/Random House, New York, 1965

GREGORY, DR GEORGE. *Essays Historical and Moral*, J. Johnson, London, 1788

GRENFELL, REV PASCOE. *Fifty Days on Board a Slave-Vessel in the Mozambique Channel*, Charles Gilpin, London, 1848

GUNTHER, JOHN. *Inside Africa*, Hamish Hamilton, London, 1955

HALLIDAY, JOHN. *The Life of William late Earl of Mansfield*, Printed for P. Elmsly, D. Bremner, T. Cadell, Jr, and W. Davies, T. Payne, and W. Clarke & Son, London; J. Cooke, Oxford; and J. Deighton, Cambridge, 1797

HOARE, PRINCE. *Memoirs of Granville Sharp*, Henry Colborn, London, 1820

HOWELL, T. B. *A Complete Collection of STATE TRIALS and Proceedings for High Treason and other Crimes and Misdemeanours from the Earliest Period to the Present Time* (vol XX, AD 1771–7), Printed by T. C. Hansard, Peterborough-Court, Fleet Street, London, 1814

KATZ, WILLIAM LOREN. *Eyewitness: The Negro in American History*, Pitman Publishing Corporation, New York, 1967

LASCELLES, E. C. P. *Granville Sharp and the Freedom of the Slaves in England*, Oxford University Press, London, 1928

Law Quarterly Review (vol 50), London, 1934

LAWRENCE, A. W. *Trade Castles and Forts of West Africa*, Jonathan Cape, London, 1963

LITTLETON, EDWARD. *The Groans of the Plantations*, M. Clark, London, 1689

LIVERPOOL, CITY OF. Custom House *Records*

Liverpool, History of (Anonymous). William Robinson, Liverpool, 1810

London Magazine (vol IX), 1740

MACKENZIE-GRIEVE, AVERIL. *Last Years of the English Slave Trade*, Putnam & Co, London, 1941

MANNIX, DANIEL P. (with MALCOLM COWLEY). *Black Cargoes*, Viking Press, New York, 1962

NEWSPAPERS. London: *Lloyd's Evening Post and British Chronicle; London Gazette; Morning Chronicle and London Advertiser; St. James's Chronicle; The Times*. Kingston, Jamaica: *Royal Gazette*. Boston, Mass: *News Letter*. (All eighteenth century)

NEWTON, JOHN. *The Journal of a Slave Trader 1750–1754*, Epworth Press, London, 1962

OLIVER, ROBERT and FAGE, J. D. *A Short History of Africa*, Penguin Books, London, 1965

PHILLIPS, ULRICH B. *American Negro Slavery*, Louisiana State University Press, Baton Rouge, La, 1966

POPE-HENNESSY, JAMES. *Sins of the Fathers*, Weidenfeld & Nicolson, London, 1967

PUBLIC RECORDS OFFICE. KB 122/484/Membrane 651—1783 ('Collingwood *versus* Gregson'); KB 122/489/Membrane 1051—1783 ('Gregson *versus* Gilbert')

RAMSAY, JAMES. *An Essay on the Treatment and Conversion of African Slaves in the Sugar Islands*, 1784

ROSCOE, HENRY. *Reports of Cases Argued and Determined in the Court of King's Bench (1782–5)* (vol III), 1831

SHARP, GRANVILLE. *The Granville Sharp Papers*, Hardwicke Court, Gloucester

TANNENBAUM, FRANK. *Slave and Citizen*, Vintage Books/Alfred A. Knopf Inc/Random House Inc, New York, 1946

WARD, W. E. F. *The Royal Navy and the Slavers*, George Allen & Unwin Ltd, London, 1969

WEISBORD, ROBERT G. 'The Case of the Slave-Ship "Zong" ', *History Today*, London, August 1969

WEST, RICHARD. *Back to Africa*, Jonathan Cape, London, 1970

WILBERFORCE, WILLIAM. *A Letter on the Abolition of the Slave Trade*, T. Cadell & W. Davies, London, 1807

WILLIAMS, GOMER. *History of the Liverpool Privateers*, Heinemann, London, and Edward Howell, Liverpool, 1897

List of Sources

CHAPTER ONE

Richard Hakluyt	*Principal Navigations* (1589)
	High Court of Admiralty, *Examinations* (vol 17)
	Winthrop Papers, Massachusetts Historical Society, Fourth series (vol VI)
	Ibid
	Calendar of State Papers, Colonial (1574–1660)
	Rhode Island Colonial Records (vol I)
	New York Colonial Documents (vol II)
	The Several Declarations of the Company of Royal Adventurers trading into Africa (1667)
	Ibid
	Calendar of State Papers, Colonial (1661–8)
	Calendar of State Papers, Colonial (1669–74)
Elizabeth Donnan	*Documents Illustrative of the History of the Slave Trade to America* (vol I) (1930)
	Ibid
	Ibid
Edward Littleton (ed)	*The Groans of the Plantations* (1689)
Thomas Phillips	*A Journal of a Voyage made in the* Hannibal *of London* (1732)
	Act of Parliament: 9 and 10 Wm III, c 26 (1698)

CHAPTER TWO

Charles Davenant	*Political and Commercial Works* (1709)
	Boston *News Letter* (10 June 1706)
	Commons Journals (1708–9) (vol XVI)
	The South Sea Company, *Minutes of the Committee of Correspondence* (1713)
	Boston *News Letter* (5 June 1721)
	Treasury Papers, *The Royal African Company: Committee Report on the State of Trade* (1721)
	Jefferies Manuscripts, Bristol Public Library
	Ibid
William Saunders (ed)	*The Colonial Records of North Carolina* (vol II) (1886)
Prince Hoare	*Memoirs of Granville Sharp* (1820)
	Boston *News Letter* (6 May 1731)
Francis Moore	*Travels into the Inland Parts of Africa* (1739)

CHAPTER THREE

	Commerce of Rhode Island (vol I)
	The Gentleman's Magazine (No X) (July 1740)
	The London Magazine (vol IX) (December 1740)
	John Bannister Letter-Book (No 66), Newport Historical Society
	Act of Parliament: V 23 Geo II, c 31 (1750)
John Newton	*The Journal of a Slave Trader 1750–1754* (1962)
	Rhode Island Colonial Records (vol VI)
	The Mercury, Newport, Rhode Island (10 March 1766)
	'Lord Mansfield and the Somersett Case', *Law Quarterly Review* (vol 50) (1934)
William Loren Katz	*Eyewitness: The Negro in American History* (1967)
	Peleg Clarke Letter Book, Newport Historical Society
	Ibid

CHAPTER FOUR

Prince Hoare	*Memoirs of Granville Sharp* (1820)
William Loren Katz	*Eyewitness: The Negro in American History* (1967)
	City of Liverpool, Municipal Archives (1700–1835)
	Act of Parliament: 28 Geo III, c 54 (1788)
	House of Commons, *Minutes of the Evidence Delivered before a Select Committee of the Whole House to Whom it Was Referred to Consider of the Slave Trade*, Parliamentary Papers (1731–1800)
	Ibid
	The Times (28 October 1791)
	Hansard (2 April 1792)

Royal Gazette, Kingston, Jamaica (20 June 1792)
Ibid (15 June 1792)
Act of Parliament: 47 Geo III, c 36 (1807)

CHAPTER FIVE

W. E. F. Ward   *The Royal Navy and the Slavers* (1969)

Globe and Traveller, London (9 December 1823)

The Liberator (22 June 1833)

Act of Parliament: Anno Tertio & Quarto, Gulielmi IV Regis, CAP. LXXIII
(28 August 1833)

H. S. Commager   *Documents of American History* (1934)

William Loren Katz   *Eyewitness: The Negro in American History* (1967)

Herbert Aptheker   *A Documentary History of the Negro People in the United States* (1965) (3 letters)

The Liberator (27 April 1860)

War Records Office, National Archives, Washington, DC

The National Archives, Washington, DC

Ibid

Acknowledgements of Illustrations

National Portrait Gallery, frontispiece, 3, 6, 22, 23, 24, 26, 27, 33, 44

United States Information Service, 1, 2, 14, 29, 32, 51, 54, 56, 57, 58, 59, 60, 61

Crown Copyright, by permission of HM Stationery Office, 4

Radio Times Hulton Picture Library, 5, 7, 12, 17, 20, 21, 28, 34, 37, 47, 49, 50, 53, 55

United Africa Company, 8, 9, 10, 11

Guildhall Library, London, 13

West India Committee, London, 15, 18, 19, 25, 36, 38, 42, 45, 46, 48, 52

Wedgwood, 30, 31

Courtauld Institute, London, 35

British Museum, 39, 40, 41, 43

Religious Society of Friends, 16

Numbers 8, 10, 15, 18, 19, 25, 36, 38, 39, 40, 41, 42, 43, 45, 46, 48 and 52 were photographed by Eileen Tweedy; and numbers 13, 16 by R. B. Fleming & Co Ltd